It is time to do some maths!

How to use this book

Do you remember how to use this **Practice Book**?

Use the **Textbook** first to learn how to solve this type of problem.

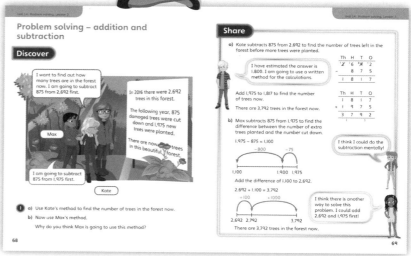

This shows you which **Textbook** page you need.

Have a go at questions by yourself using this **Practice Book**. Use what you have learnt.

Challenge questions make you think hard!

Questions with this light bulb make you think differently.

Power Maths

Year 6 Practice Book 6C

Did you use any maths in real life during the holiday?

Write down what maths you found useful.

This book belongs to _____ .

My class is _____ .

Pearson

Contents

This looks like a good challenge!

2

Reflect

Each lesson ends with a Reflect question so you can think about what you have learnt.

Use My Power Points at the back of this book to keep track of what you have learnt.

Reflect

Draw and label a bar model to match the problem in question 4.

53

My journal

At the end of a unit your teacher will ask you to fill in My journal.

This will help you show how much you can do now that you have finished the unit.

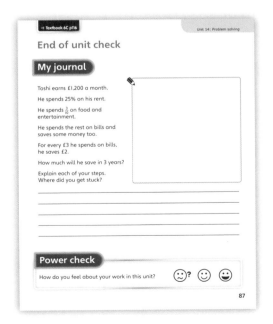

→ Textbook 6C p116

Unit 14: Problem solving

End of unit check

My journal

Toshi earns £1,200 a month.

He spends 25% on his rent.

He spends $\frac{3}{10}$ on food and entertainment.

He spends the rest on bills and saves some money too.

For every £3 he spends on bills, he saves £2.

How much will he save in 3 years?

Explain each of your steps. Where did you get stuck?

Power check

How do you feel about your work in this unit?

87

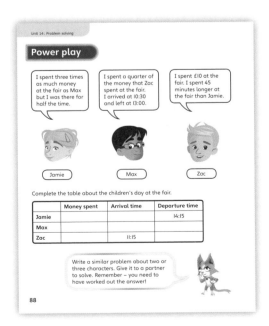

Unit 14: Problem solving

Power play

I spent three times as much money at the fair as Max but I was there for half the time.

I spent a quarter of the money that Zac spent at the fair. I arrived at 10:30 and left at 13:00.

I spent £10 at the fair. I spent 45 minutes longer at the fair than Jamie.

Jamie

Max

Zac

Complete the table about the children's day at the fair.

	Money spent	Arrival time	Departure time
Jamie			14:15
Max			
Zac		11:15	

Write a similar problem about two or three characters. Give it to a partner to solve. Remember – you need to have worked out the answer!

88

→ Textbook 6C p8

Measuring with a protractor

1 Complete the measurements accurately.

a)

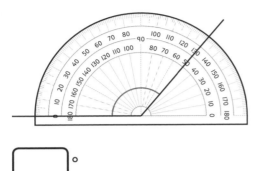

[ ] °

c)

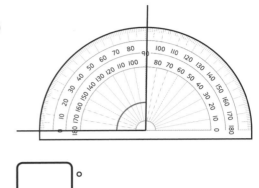

[ ] °

b)

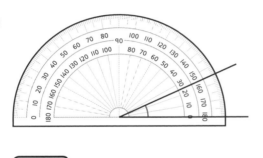

[ ] °

d)

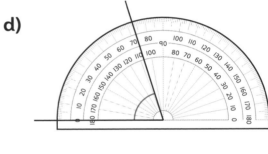

[ ] °

2 Draw lines to match each angle with the correct measurement.

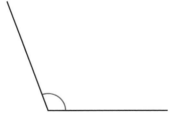
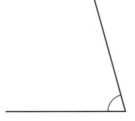

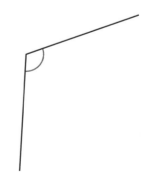

| 75° | 113° | 72° | 110° |

3 **a)** Measure and label all of the interior angles.

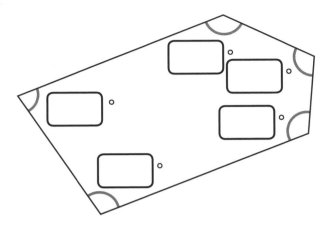 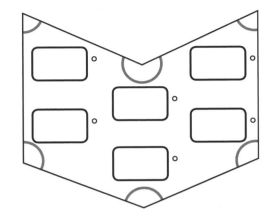

b) Which one of the following is a regular shape? Explain your answer.

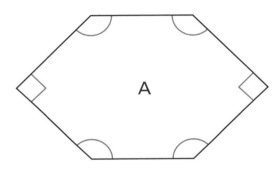 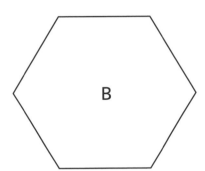

A   B

_____

_____

4 Mo says, 'These angles increase in size.' Is he correct? Explain your answer.

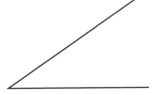 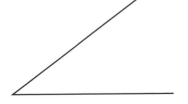

_____

_____

7

5 Complete each symmetric figure. Measure and label all the interior angles.

a)

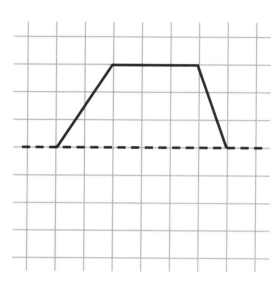

b)

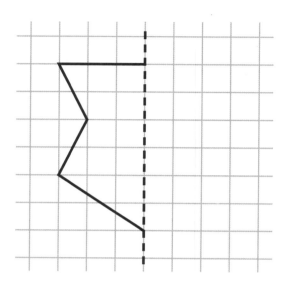

Explain what you notice.

_____

_____

Reflect

What simple mistakes might be made when measuring angles?
Write a checklist for avoiding these mistakes.

 _____

 _____

_____

Drawing shapes accurately

1 Draw these three angles. In each case, the first line has been drawn for you.

a) 60°   **b)** 70°   **c)** 80°

2 Use the space below to draw this shape accurately.

Find and label the missing measurements to the nearest degree and cm.

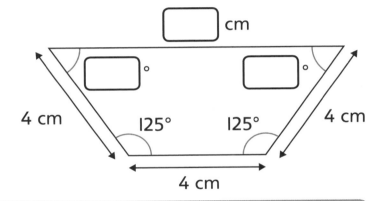

3 Complete the three parallelograms, ensuring the angles and lengths are correct.

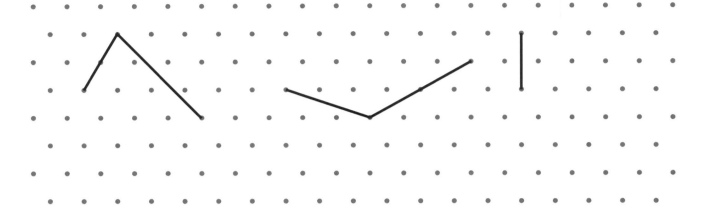

4 Two lines of three different kites have been drawn. Complete the kites.

5 Draw accurately a kite, a rhombus and a rectangle.

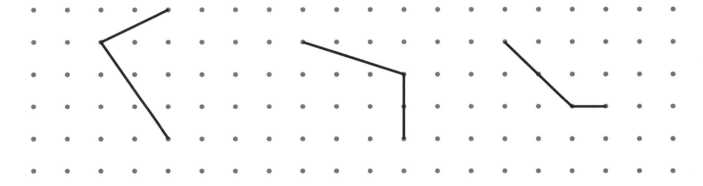

6 One side of each of two rectangles has been drawn.

Each rectangle has an area of 12 cm². Complete the rectangles by drawing the sides and angles accurately.

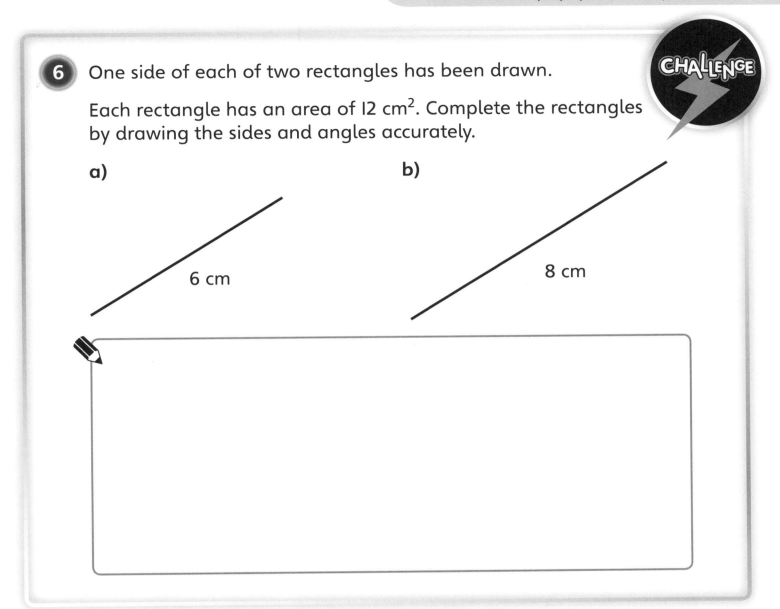

a)

6 cm

b)

8 cm

Reflect

Lee is drawing a 100° angle. What are the steps he needs to take? What mistakes does he need to avoid?

→ Textbook 6C p16

Angles in triangles

1 **a)** Circle all the angles that have been incorrectly measured.

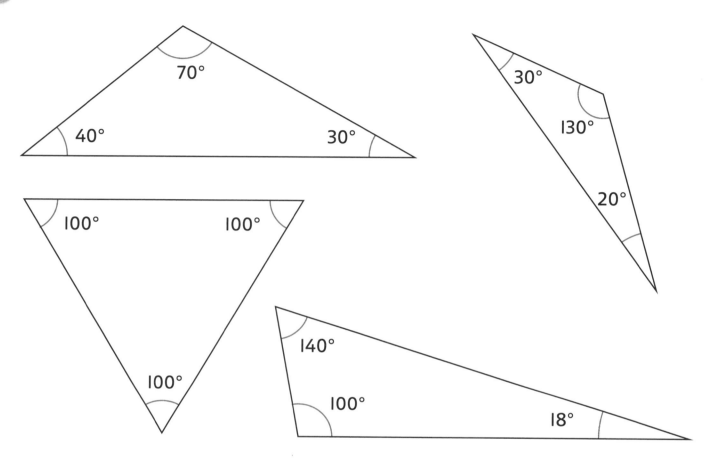

b) Draw this triangle accurately and then measure the missing angle.

not to scale

2 The corners from these paper triangles have been torn off. Draw lines to match the angles to the triangles they are from.

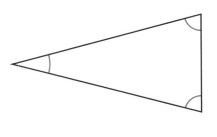

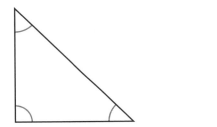

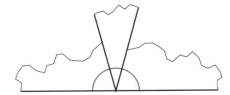

3 Tick to show which statements are always true, sometimes true and never true. Discuss your answers with your partner.

A triangle has ...	Always true	Sometimes true	Never true
... three acute angles.			
... two right angles.			
... a right angle and an obtuse angle.			
... three different angles.			
... angles that add up to 180°.			
... at least two acute angles.			

4 In each circle, join three dots to form a different triangle. Measure and write the measurements of all of the angles in the triangles and check that they add up to 180° in each triangle.

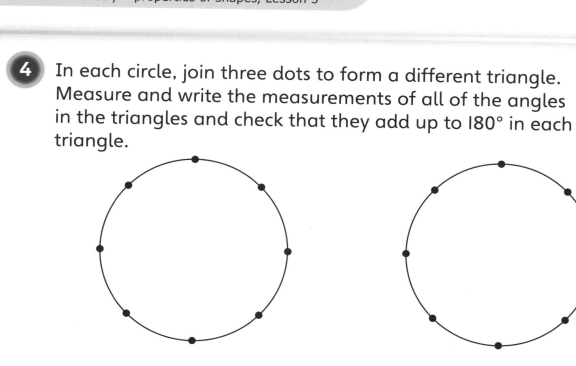

CHALLENGE

Reflect

What is the sum of the angles in a triangle? How do you know? How can you prove it?

Angles in triangles ❷

1 Calculate the missing angles.

a)

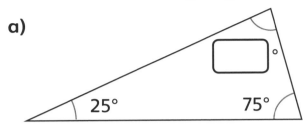

c)

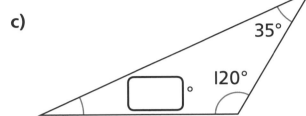

b)

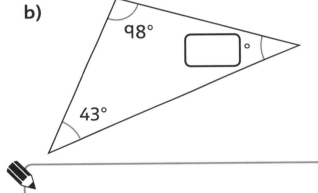

d)

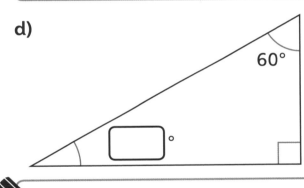

2 Measure two angles and then calculate the third, showing your calculation.

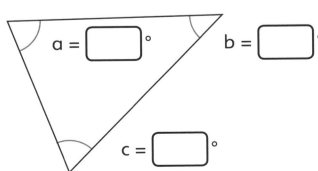

3 Calculate the size of the angles p, q and r.

Angle q is twice as big as angle r.

Angle r is three times as big as angle p.

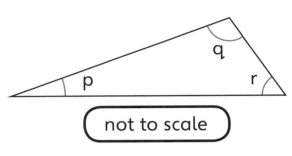

not to scale

180°

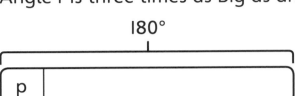

p

4 Draw lines to match groups of three angles that could form a triangle.

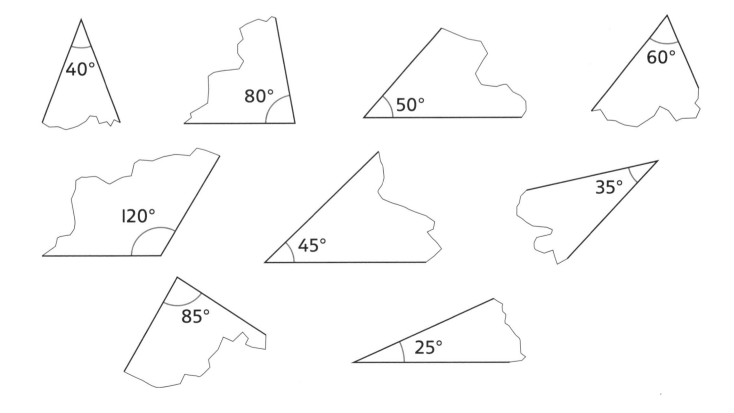

40°

80°

50°

60°

120°

45°

35°

85°

25°

5 Calculate the missing angles.

CHALLENGE

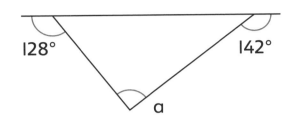

128° 142° a

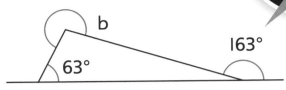

b 163° 63°

a = ⬚ °

b = ⬚ °

The triangle has been drawn in a rectangle.

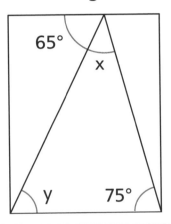

65° x y 75°

x = ⬚ ° y = ⬚ °

Reflect

Draw two different diagrams for triangles with a missing angle of 50 degrees. How did you work out the angles for the triangles?

17

→ Textbook 6C p24

Angles in triangles ③

1 Use the information about the angles to mark the equal lengths, using the correct notation.

a)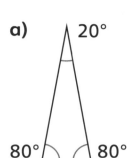
20°
80° 80°

b)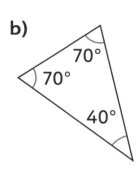
70°
70°
40°

c)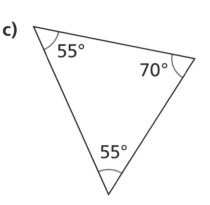
55°
70°
55°

d)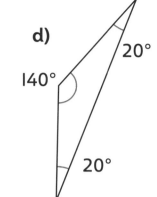
20°
140°
20°

2 Calculate the missing angles in each triangle below.

a)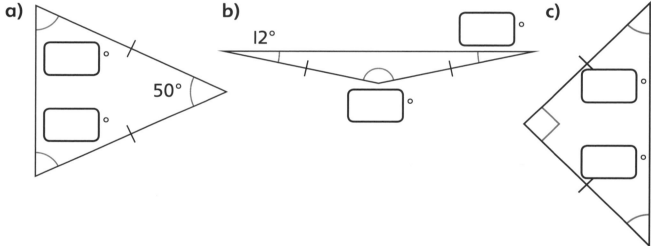
☐°
50°
☐°

b)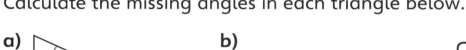
12°
☐°
☐°

c)
☐°
☐°

3 Tick the isosceles triangle and mark both the equal lengths and the equal angles.

4 Amelia draws an isosceles triangle. One of her angles is 56°.

Bella draws an isosceles triangle. One of her angles is 156°.

What are the other two angles in each of the triangles?

> There are two solutions to mine.
>
> Amelia

> There must be two solutions to mine too.
>
> Bella

Do you agree with them? How many solutions can you find?
Explain your answer using diagrams with correct markings.

5 Calculate all of the missing angles below.

CHALLENGE

a)

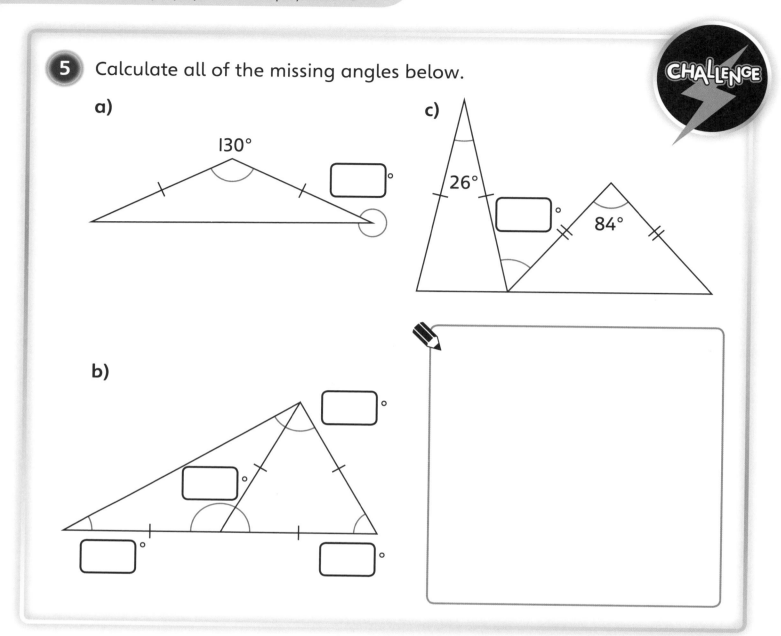

b)

Reflect

Create a missing angle problem involving isosceles triangles.

Angles in polygons ❶

1 Join each shape to the correct label.

a)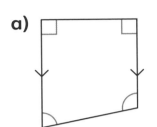

b)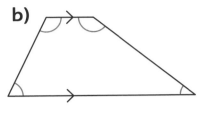

c)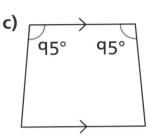
95°   95°

d)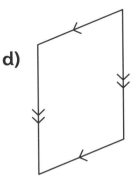

Parallelogram	Isosceles trapezium	Scalene trapezium	Right-angled trapezium

2 The following shapes have been made from rectangles. Calculate the missing angles.

a)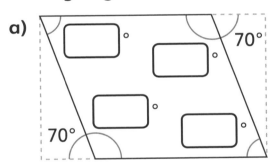
70°
70°

b)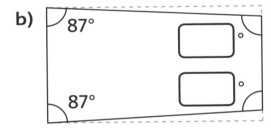
87°
87°

3 Add markings to show any parallel lines or equal lengths in the shapes below.

a)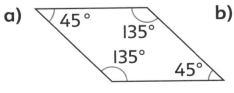
45°
135°
135°
45°

b)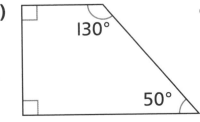
130°
50°

c)
135° 135°
45°   45°

4 Calculate the missing angles.

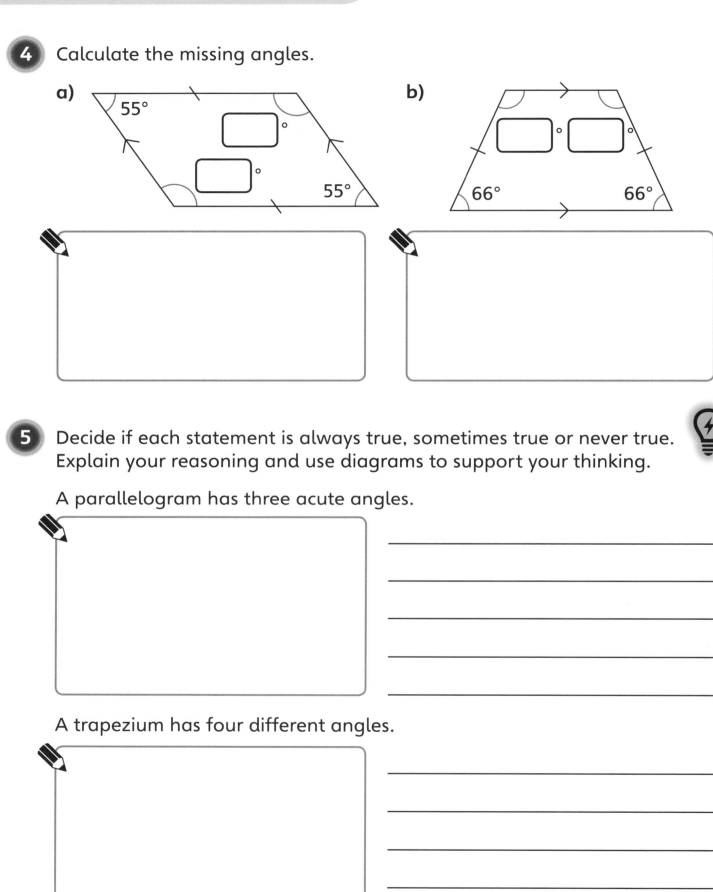

a)

55°

55°

b)

66°   66°

5 Decide if each statement is always true, sometimes true or never true. Explain your reasoning and use diagrams to support your thinking.

A parallelogram has three acute angles.

_____

_____

_____

_____

_____

A trapezium has four different angles.

_____

_____

_____

_____

_____

6 **a)** How many different parallelograms can you create on these grids?

CHALLENGE

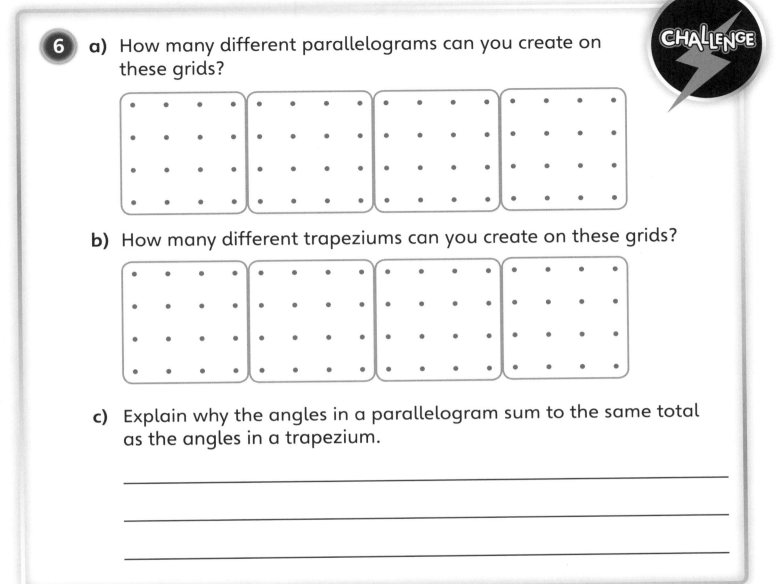

b) How many different trapeziums can you create on these grids?

c) Explain why the angles in a parallelogram sum to the same total as the angles in a trapezium.

_____

_____

_____

Reflect

Draw a diagram to explain what you know about the angle sums in trapeziums and parallelograms.

→ Textbook 6C p32

Angles in polygons ❷

1 Calculate the missing angle of each shape.

a)

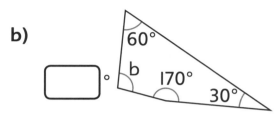

c)
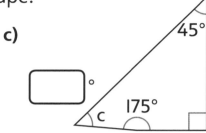
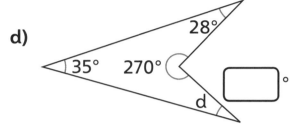

b)
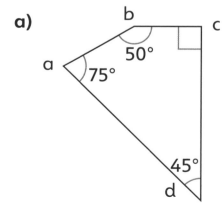

d)
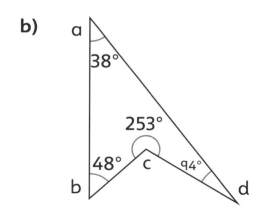

2 In each shape one angle has been labelled incorrectly. Identify this angle and calculate its correct value.

a)

b
c
50°
a
75°
45°
d

b)

a
38°
253°
48°   c   94°
b   d

3 Draw lines to split each shape into triangles. Write the angle total for each shape.

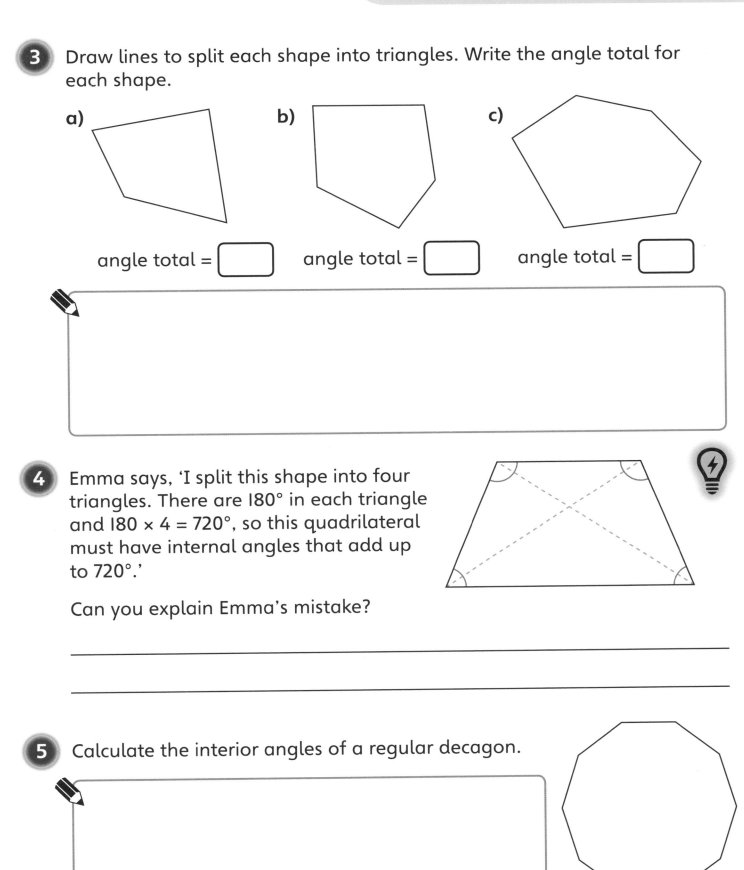

a)

angle total = ☐

b)

angle total = ☐

c)

angle total = ☐

4 Emma says, 'I split this shape into four triangles. There are 180° in each triangle and 180 × 4 = 720°, so this quadrilateral must have internal angles that add up to 720°.'

Can you explain Emma's mistake?

_____

_____

5 Calculate the interior angles of a regular decagon.

angle total = ☐   each interior angle = ☐

25

6

a) The regular hexagon has been drawn inside a rectangle.

Calculate angles a and b.

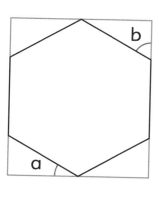

b) How many angles can you calculate in this diagram of a pentagon drawn inside a rectangle? Write the angle measurements on the shape.

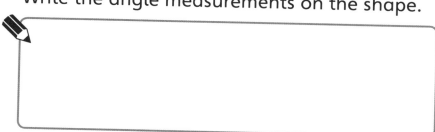

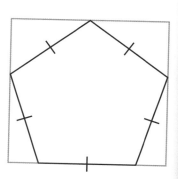

Reflect

Create a missing angle problem involving a quadrilateral. The missing angle should be 40°.

Vertically opposite angles

1 Draw lines to match each diagram with the missing angle.

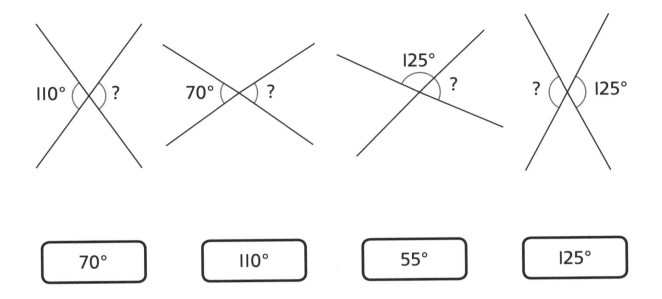

| 70° | 110° | 55° | 125° |

2 Circle the diagram that does **not** show vertically opposite angles.

3 Calculate each of the missing angles below.

a)

b)

c)

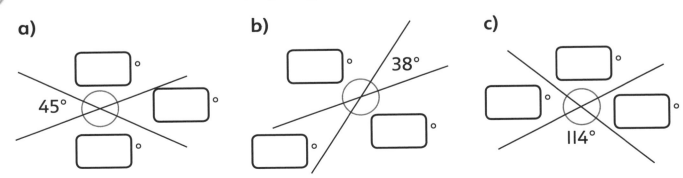

4 Draw a line so that there are two 135° angles.

5 Complete the table below.

Experiment 1 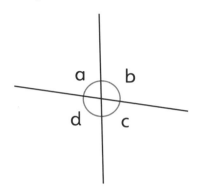 Experiment 2 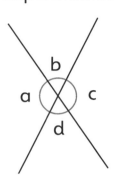 Experiment 3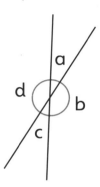

In Experiment 1, angle a is 20° less than angle b.

In Experiment 2, angle a is twice as large as angle b.

In Experiment 3, angle a is one fifth the size of angle d.

	Angle a	Angle b	Angle c	Angle d
Experiment 1				
Experiment 2				
Experiment 3				

6 Calculate the missing angles.

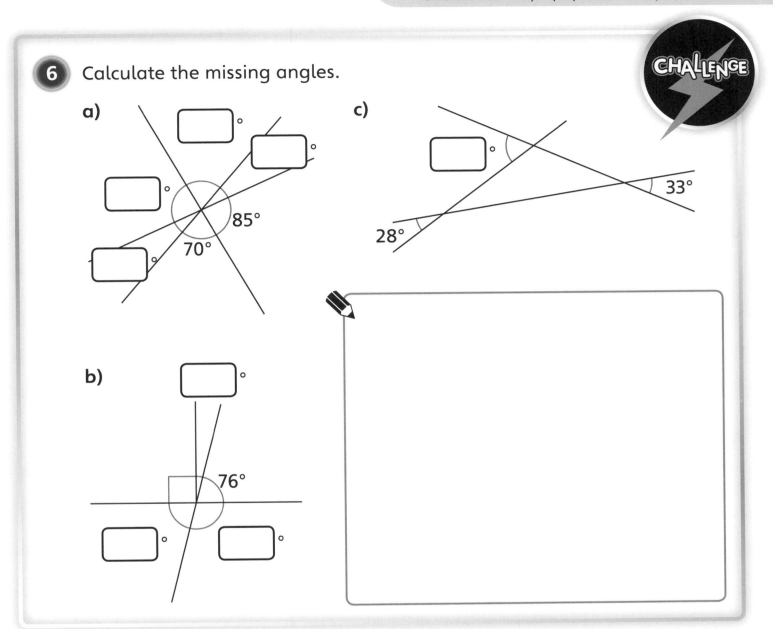

CHALLENGE

a)

85°
70°

b)

76°

c)

33°
28°

Reflect

Describe in words why vertically opposite angles must be equal.

Equal distance

1 Draw 20 dots, each one exactly 25 mm from the cross.

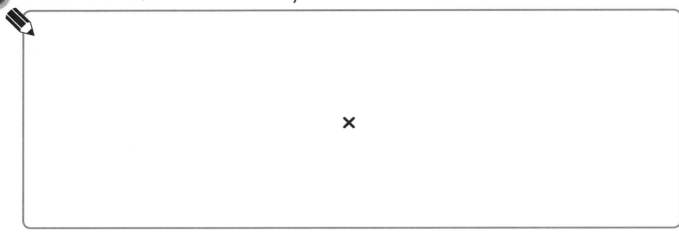

Complete the sentence.
The dots are on a circle with a radius of ☐ mm.

2 Label whether each diagram shows the radius or the diameter. Measure and write the radius and diameter for each circle.

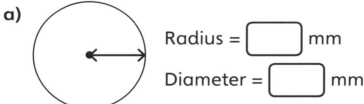

a)

Radius = ☐ mm

Diameter = ☐ mm

b)

Radius = ☐ mm

Diameter = ☐ mm

c)

Radius = ☐ mm

Diameter = ☐ mm

3 Tick the statements that are true.

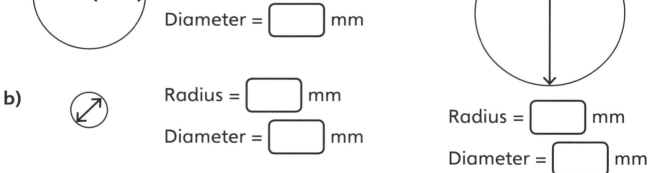

The radius is twice as long as the diameter. ☐

The diameter passes through the centre of the circle. ☐

If the radius is x, then the diameter is x + x. ☐

4 Calculate the radius of each circle.

a)

8 mm

b)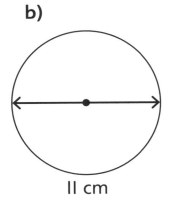

11 cm

c)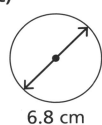

6.8 cm

d)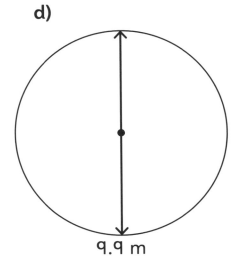

9.9 m

Not to scale

a) Radius =

☐ mm

b) Radius =

☐ cm

c) Radius =

☐ cm

d) Radius =

☐ m

5 **a)** Calculate the radius of a 2p coin.

Coins not actual size

13 cm

Radius = ☐ mm

b) This is a 5p coin.

Calculate the length of the line.

18 mm

The line is ☐ mm

6 **a)** The perimeter of the triangle is 16·8 cm.
What is the radius of one of the circles?

CHALLENGE

b) Draw a parallelogram with a
perimeter of 19·6 cm.

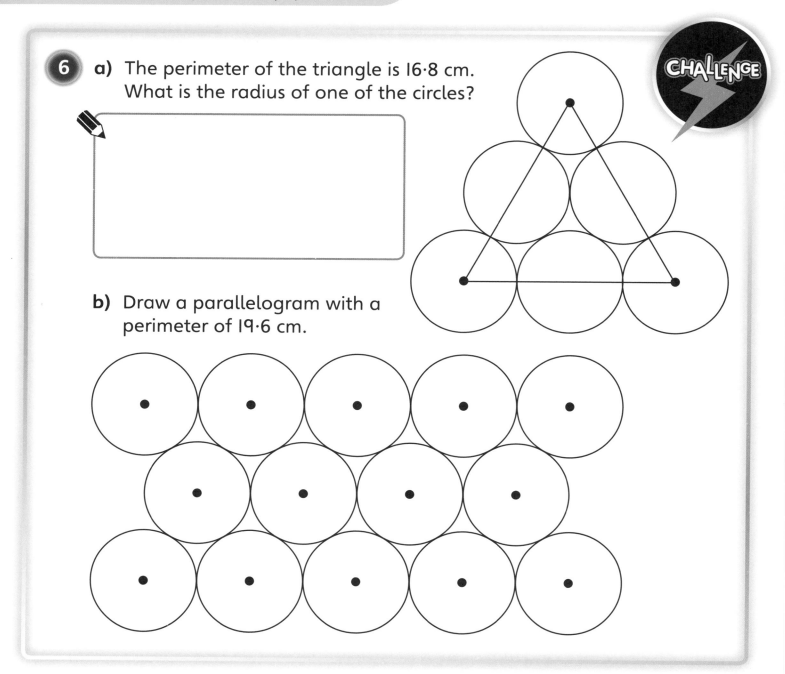

Reflect

Describe how to draw a circle with a diameter of 4 cm.

Parts of a circle

1 Tick the diagram that has been labelled correctly.

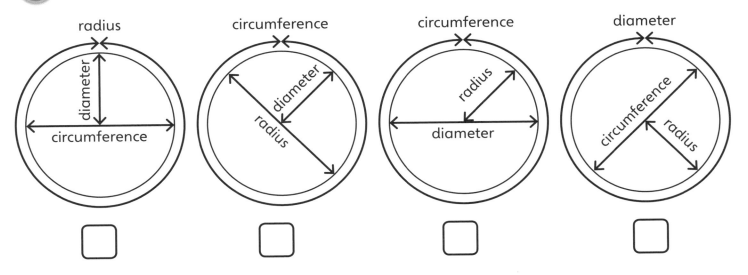

2 **a)** On each circle draw two dots on the circumference. Then join these dots to the centre to form triangles. Measure one angle in each triangle and then calculate the other angles.

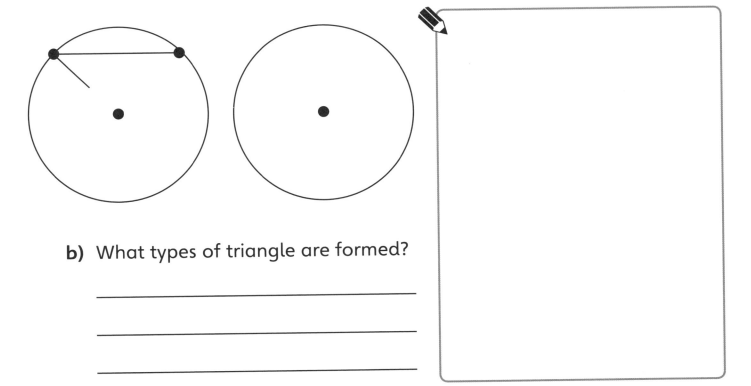

b) What types of triangle are formed?

_____

_____

_____

3 Join dots to form different quadrilaterals. Try to form: a parallelogram, an isosceles trapezium, a rhombus and a kite.

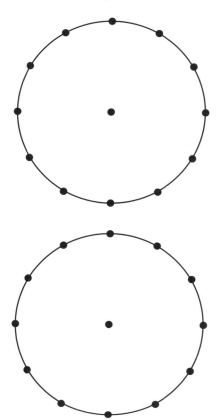

4 Form a triangle using the diameter and a point on the circumference. Work out the angles of the triangle. You should only need to measure one of the angles.

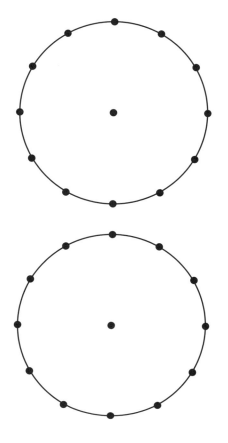

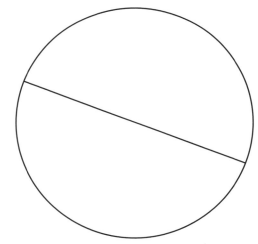

You do not need to measure the right angle.

5 Find the approximate area of this circle.

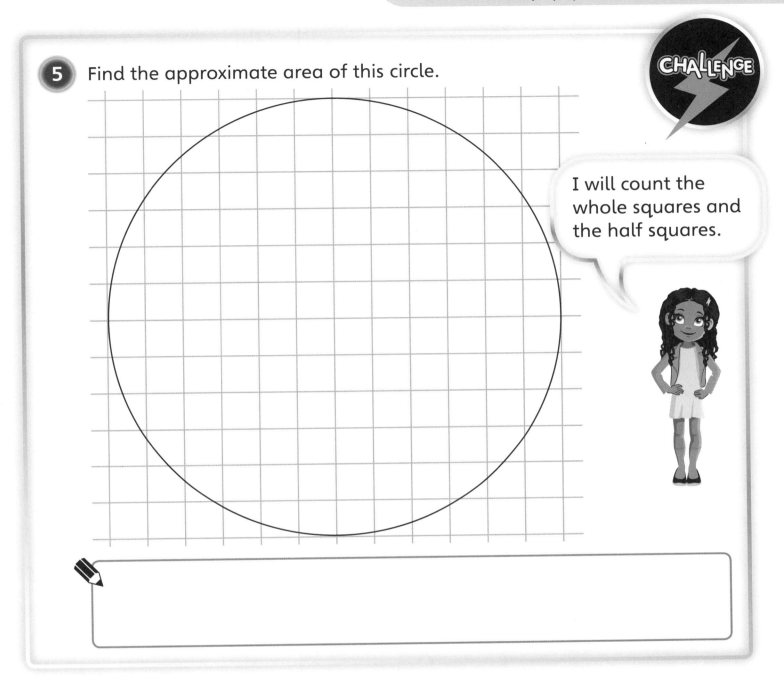

CHALLENGE

I will count the whole squares and the half squares.

Reflect

Describe how to use a circle to draw an isosceles triangle.

→ Textbook 6C p48

Nets ❶

① Draw lines to match the nets to the 3D shapes.

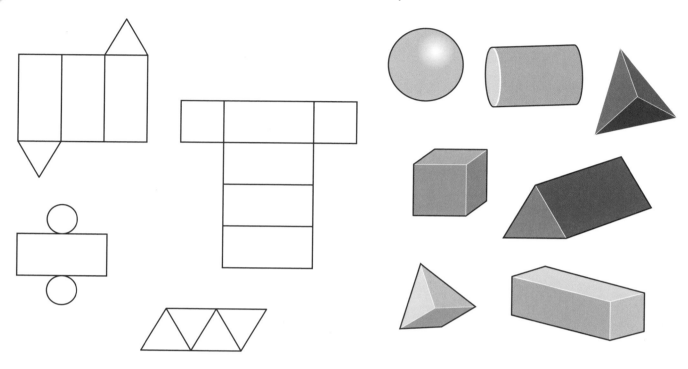

② Tick any nets that will fold correctly to form a pyramid.

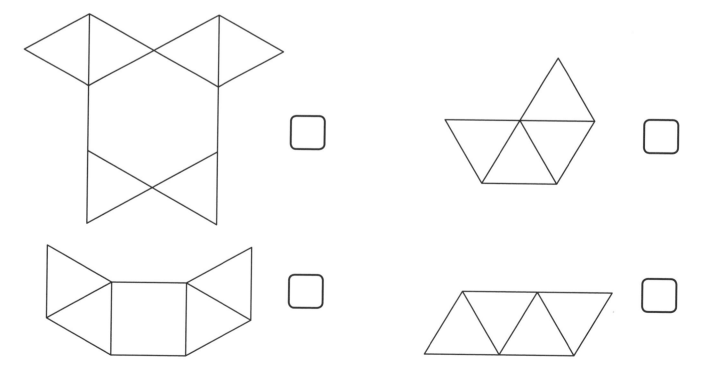

3 This net forms a hexagonal prism. The shapes on the faces should be in pairs on opposite faces. Draw one more dot, one more triangle and one more square so that there are pairs of shapes on opposite faces of the prism.

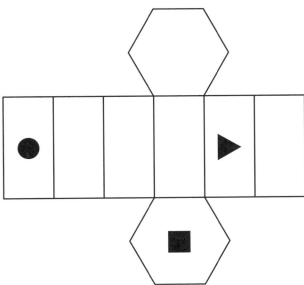

4 The top half of this cuboid is painted, and the bottom half is white. Complete the shading on the net.

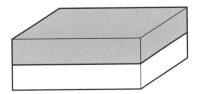
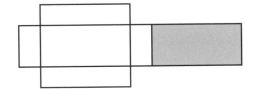

5 Complete the net of the cuboid.

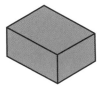

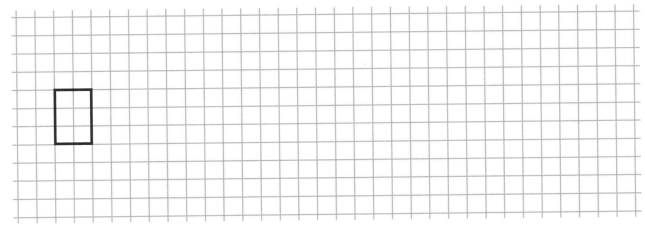

6 Colour or shade this net so that the same colours or shading never touch when it is folded to form a hexagonal prism.

(Colours or shading are allowed to touch at a vertex.)

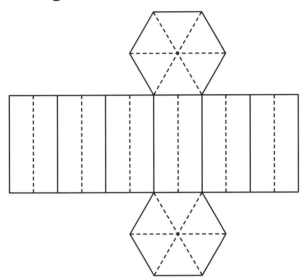

Reflect

Draw a net for a pyramid.

Nets ②

1 Tick the nets that will form a cube.

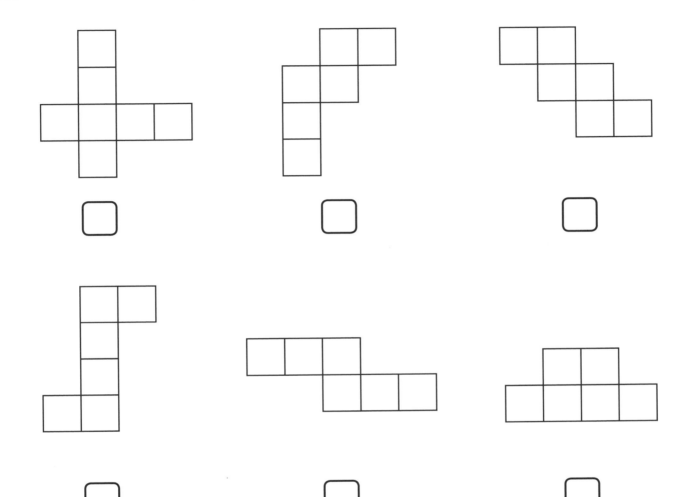

2 Complete the net of the cube in three different ways.

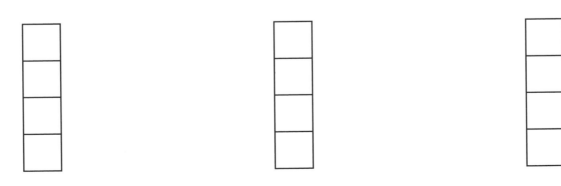

3 On this cube, three faces have an animal on them that begins with the letter on the opposite face.

Draw three possible nets for this cube.

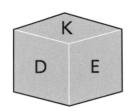

4 Complete the shading on the net for this cube.

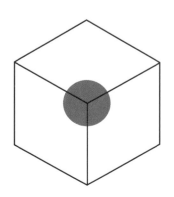

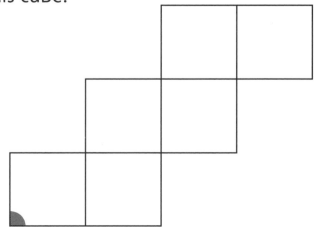

5 Here is a net of a cube. What is the volume of the cube?

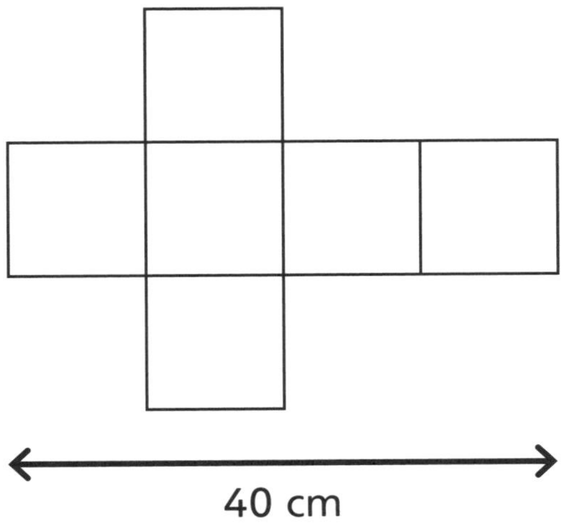

CHALLENGE

Not to scale

← 40 cm →

Reflect

Provide some advice for how to spot if a net will form a cube.

End of unit check

My journal

1 Two straight lines cross a square.

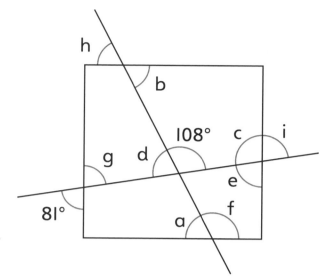

Which other angles can you work out?

Explain how you worked them out.

_____

_____

_____

_____

_____

_____

_____

2 Write the correct label under each net.

Cube   Prism   Pyramid   Does not make
                                               a 3D shape

A 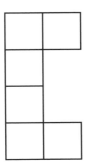   C 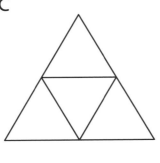   E 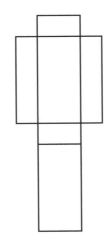   G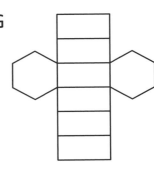

_____   _____   _____   _____

B 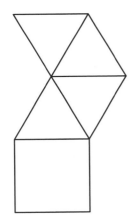   D 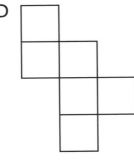   F 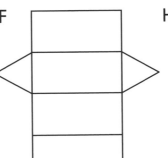   H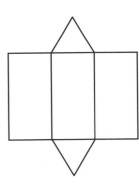

_____   _____   _____   _____

Power check

How do you feel about your work in this unit?

Power puzzle

Cut a rectangle into 8 triangles like this.

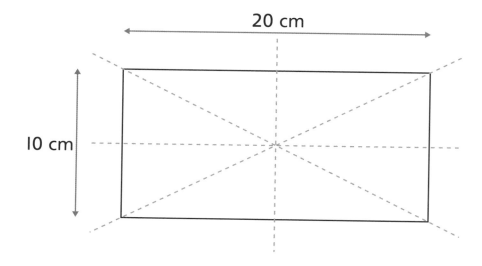

20 cm

10 cm

How many different polygons can you make? Try using:

4 triangles   5 triangles   6 triangles   7 triangles   8 triangles

Now sort your shapes depending on features such as symmetry, or the number of obtuse angles.

Problem solving – place value

1 The table shows children's scores for a computer game.

Add names to make each statement correct.

Max	57,483
Emma	56,832
Jamilla	57,843
Richard	56,809

a) Max's score < _____

b) _____ < Emma's score

c) _____ < _____ < _____ < _____

2 Four numbers have been placed in the sorting circles.

Complete the label for each group.

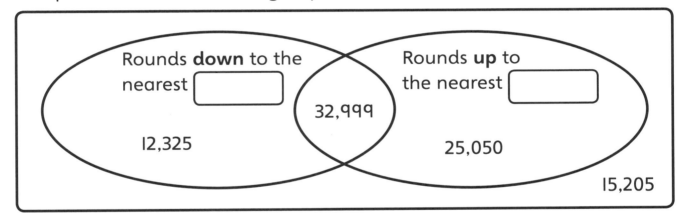

Rounds **down** to the nearest ☐

Rounds **up** to the nearest ☐

32,999

12,325

25,050

15,205

3 Aki has some digit cards. He uses the cards to make a 4-digit odd number that is greater than 6,800 but less than 9,000.

3   6   7   9

What could Aki's number be? Find all the possible answers.

4 The line graph shows the money made each day by a toy shop in a week. The numbers on the scale are missing.

Use the graph to complete the table. Label the scale to help you.

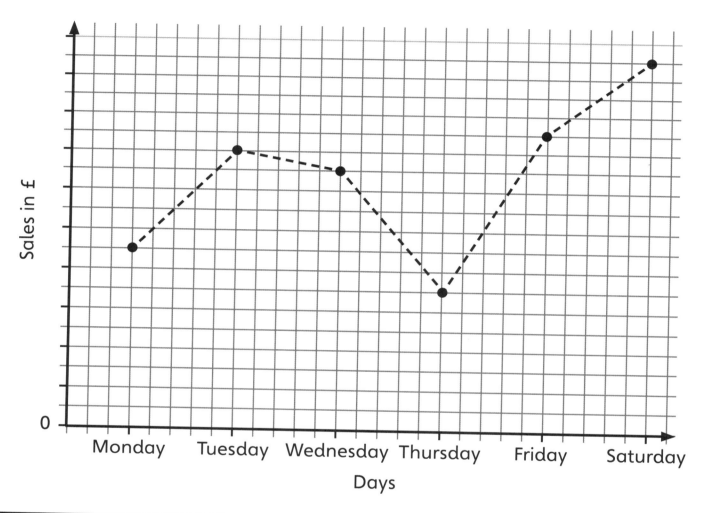

Sales in £

0

Monday   Tuesday   Wednesday   Thursday   Friday   Saturday

Days

Days	Monday	Tuesday	Wednesday	Thursday	Friday	Saturday
Sales in £	1,800					

The scale is just like a number line.
I wonder what each interval represents.

46

5 The population of City X rounds to 483,000 to the nearest 1,000.

The population of City Y rounds to 480,000 to the nearest 10,000.

Jamie says, 'The population of City X must be larger because 483,000 is larger than 480,000.'

Do you agree? Explain your answer.

CHALLENGE

I'm going to think about rules for rounding to help me.

_____

_____

_____

_____

Reflect

Write one more number in each section of the sorting circles.

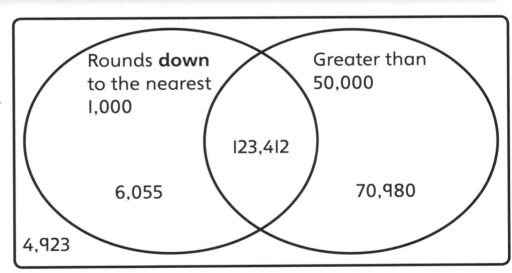

Rounds **down** to the nearest 1,000

Greater than 50,000

123,412

6,055

70,980

4,923

Explain the position of 123,412 in the sorting circles.

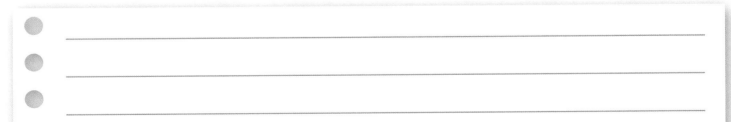

→ Textbook 6C p64

Problem solving – negative numbers

1 Tick the pair of numbers that has the biggest difference.

a) ⁻4 and 12

b) ⁻8 and 9

c) ⁻20 and ⁻11

2 a) This sequence increases by 7 each time.

What are the missing numbers?

☐ , ⁻16, ☐ , ⁻2, ☐ , ☐

b) Another sequence decreases by the same amount each time.

What are the missing numbers?

19, ☐ , 7, ☐ , ⁻5, ☐

c) What is the 10th number in the sequence in part **b)**? ☐

3 This graph shows the temperature in six cities on one day in January.

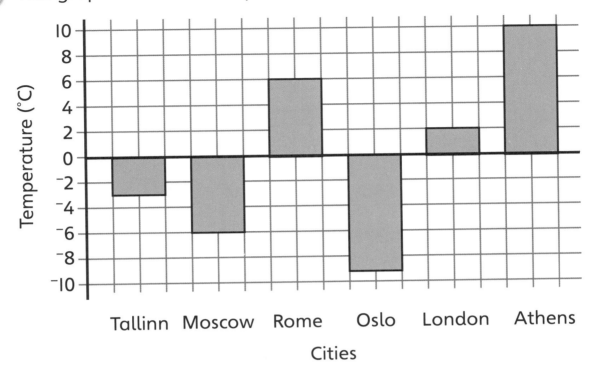

a) Which city was 5 °C warmer than Tallinn? _____

b) Which two cities have a difference in temperature of 11 °C?

_____

4 The number line shows a winter temperature and a summer temperature in Alaska.

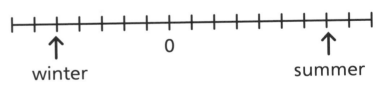

winter   summer

The difference between the temperatures is 48 degrees.

What are the temperatures?

winter temperature = [ ] °C   summer temperature = [ ] °C

49

5 Work out the missing numbers on this number line.

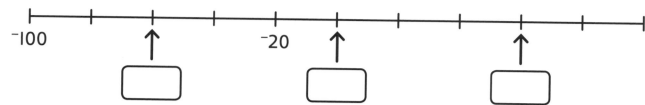

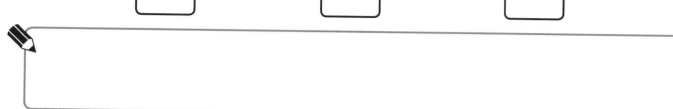

6 Arrange the numbers in the diagram so that the difference between pairs joined by a horizontal line ——— is 16 and the difference between pairs joined by a dotted vertical line ⋮ is 9.

⁻20   5   ⁻13

⁻4   3   ⁻11

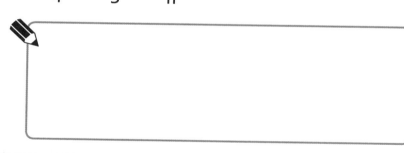

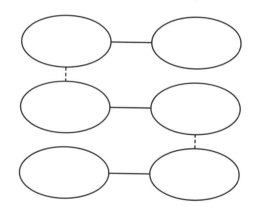

Reflect

Explain how to work out the half-way point between 24 and ⁻40.

_____

_____

_____

Problem solving – addition and subtraction

1 On Tuesday morning, the number of visitors at an adventure park is 2,365. In the afternoon, 1,790 more visitors arrive but 945 go home.

How many visitors are in the park now?

2 Max adds three numbers together. The total is 20,000.

The first number is 4,588. The second number is 12,375.

What is the third number?

3 The bar chart shows the number of visitors at the adventure park over a weekend.

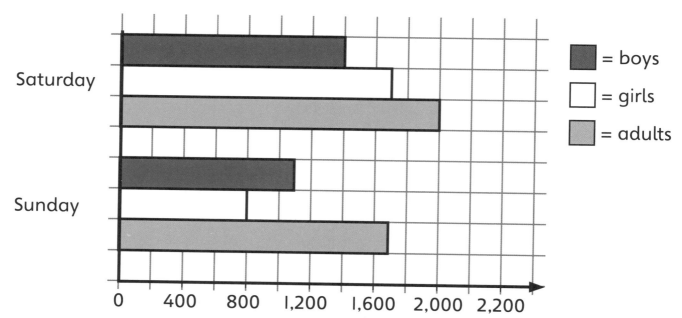

Saturday

Sunday

0   400   800   1,200   1,600   2,000   2,200

= boys

= girls

= adults

a) How many more children than adults visited the park on Saturday?

b) What is the difference between the total number of children who visited the park on Saturday and Sunday?

4 The Brown family sell cakes at the local fair. In the morning they sell 117 cakes.

In the afternoon they sell 48 fewer cakes.

How many cakes do they sell in total?

5 Write the missing digits to make these calculations correct.

a)

H	T	O	·	Tth	Hth
	5	3	·		9
+		7	·	8	2
1	3	2	·	0	

b)

Th	H	T	O
	9		7
−	6	1		3
		9	1	8

6 Find the value of each shape.

$1{,}250 - \triangle + \triangle = \pentagon$

$1{,}000 + \triangle = 1{,}600 - \square$

$700 = \square + \square$

I wonder which shape it is easiest to work out first.

CHALLENGE

$\triangle = \boxed{}$ $\square = \boxed{}$ $\pentagon = \boxed{}$

Reflect

Draw and label a bar model to match the problem in question 4.

→ **Textbook 6C p72**

Problem solving – four operations

1 Entry to a castle costs £6·50 more for adults than for children.

The cost for a family with one adult and four children is £49.

What is the cost of each ticket?

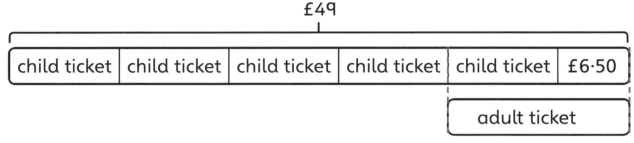

2 A supermarket needs to deliver 270 online shopping orders.

A van can carry 25 orders at a time.

How many van trips are needed to deliver all the orders?

3 A supermarket sells mixed bags of 6 lemons and 4 limes.

There are 255 lemons and 171 limes to be put into bags.

a) How many mixed bags of lemons and limes can be made?

b) How many more lemons and limes are needed to complete another bag?

4 Cups hold 0·25 l of water. Mugs hold 375 ml of water.

Jen fills 5 cups and 5 mugs with water.

How much more water does she use altogether for the mugs than for the cups?

5 A number is multiplied by 6 and then divided by 3.

20 is added to the result.

Reena says, 'That is the same as doubling the number and adding 20.'

Explain why Reena is correct. Use examples to help you.

_____

_____

_____

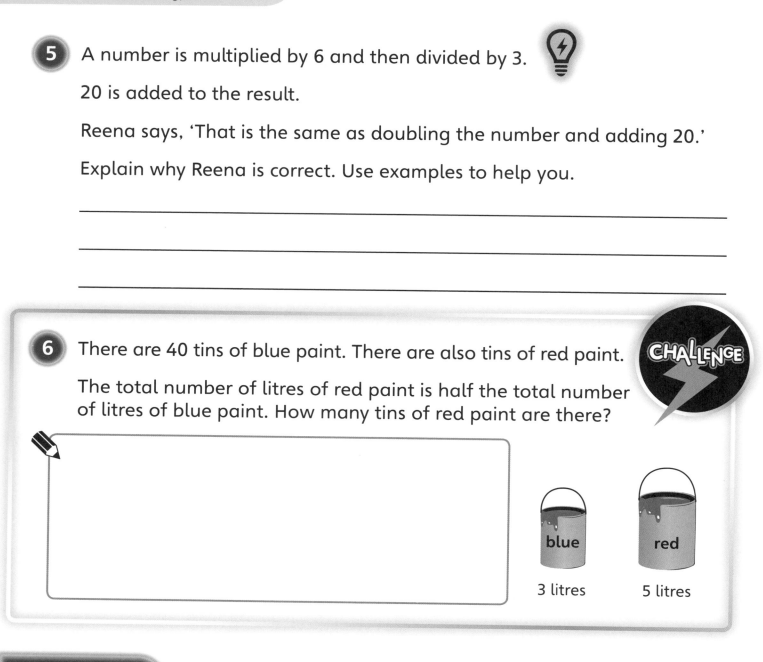

6 There are 40 tins of blue paint. There are also tins of red paint.

The total number of litres of red paint is half the total number of litres of blue paint. How many tins of red paint are there?

CHALLENGE

blue
3 litres

red
5 litres

Reflect

Write down three things you should do when solving problems.

_____

_____

_____

Problem solving – four operations ❷

1 Jamie makes bracelets using laces and different beads.

Each lace costs 25p.

This bracelet costs £1·30 to make.
The plain beads cost 18p each.
What is the cost of one spotty bead?

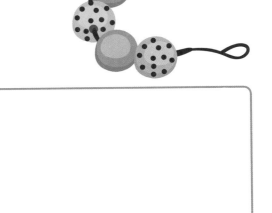

2 A tower is made with two different-sized blocks.

Calculate the height of the tower.

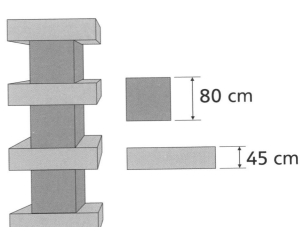

80 cm

45 cm

3 Richard compares the capacity of large and small bottles.

The capacity of a large bottle is 720 ml.

a) What is the capacity of a small bottle?

b) How many more litres of water fill 10 large bottles than 10 small bottles?

4 Alex uses these four digits to make a calculation: 3   4   8   9

Her answer is an odd multiple of 5.

What calculation did she make?
Find more than one solution.

$$\boxed{}\boxed{} \times \boxed{} + \boxed{} = \boxed{}$$

$$\boxed{}\boxed{} \times \boxed{} + \boxed{} = \boxed{}$$

$$\boxed{}\boxed{} \times \boxed{} + \boxed{} = \boxed{}$$

5 Find the diameters of the different-sized circles.

CHALLENGE

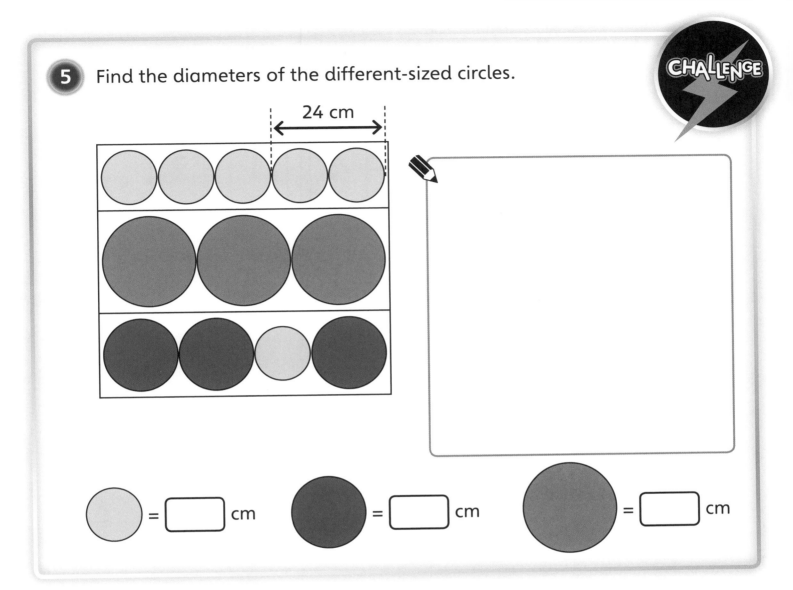

24 cm

◯ = ⬚ cm   ● = ⬚ cm   ● = ⬚ cm

Reflect

Compare the strategy you used to solve question **3 b)** with a partner's strategy.

Try your strategies to find out how many more litres of water fill 25 large bottles than 25 small bottles.

→ Textbook 6C p80

Problem solving – fractions

1 Use all the digit cards to make fractions that complete the statement.

$$\frac{\Box}{\Box} < \frac{1}{2} < \frac{\Box}{\Box}$$

| 6 | 4 | 3 | 2 |

2 Zac and Jamilla made 108 cookies to sell for charity.

Zac sold $\frac{4}{9}$ of the cookies. Jamilla sold $\frac{1}{3}$ of the cookies.

a) How many cookies did they sell altogether?

b) What fraction of the cookies were left?

3 What fraction of the rectangle is **not** shaded?

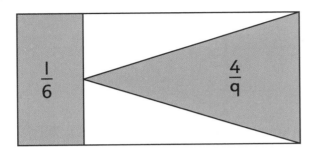

4 The distance between A and B is $1\frac{1}{4}$ km.

The distance between A and C is $4\frac{3}{5}$ km.

What is the distance from B to C?

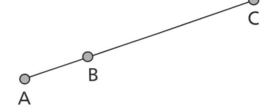

5 In a bag of marbles, 38 are green and 22 are red.

The remaining $\frac{3}{8}$ of the marbles are yellow.

How many marbles are in the bag altogether?

6 Use both the digits 3 and 4 to make the largest possible answer to each calculation.

$$\frac{\boxed{}}{8} \times \frac{2}{\boxed{}} = \boxed{}$$

$$\frac{\boxed{}}{5} + \frac{\boxed{}}{4} = \boxed{}$$

$$\frac{\boxed{}}{10} + \boxed{} = \boxed{}$$

I think I need to work out the answer each time.

I think I can use my reasoning skills to make decisions.

Reflect

$\frac{3}{8}$ $\frac{6}{14}$ $\frac{7}{12}$ $\frac{4}{9}$

Which of these fractions are larger than $\frac{1}{2}$? Use reasoning to explain your answer.

_____

_____

_____

Problem solving – decimals

1 The mass of a bag of sweets is 0·3 kg.

The mass of 5 bags of popcorn is equal to the mass of 3 bags of sweets.

What is the mass of 1 bag of popcorn?

2 **a)** 4 bags of popcorn cost £7·20.

2 bags of popcorn and a carton of juice cost £4·25.

How much does the carton of juice cost?

b) How much more does it cost to buy 8 bags of popcorn than 8 cartons of juice?

3 Write the missing numbers on the number line.

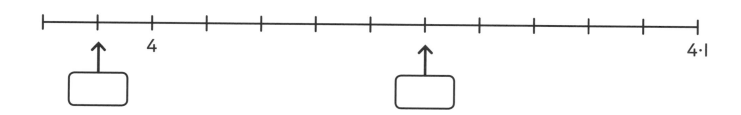

4   4·1

4

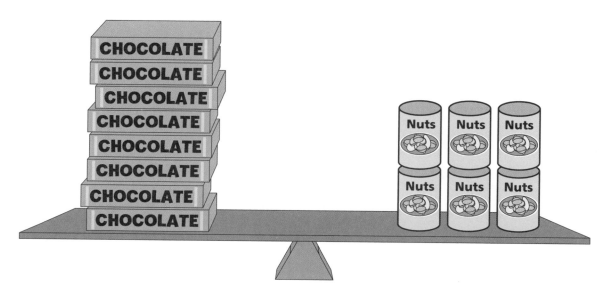

The mass of 1 bar of chocolate is 0·2 kg.

What is the mass of 1 tin of nuts?

5 Arrange the numbers in the grid so that each row, column and diagonal has the same total.

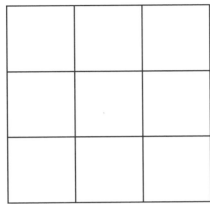

7·1   4·8   5·3

4·6   5·7   6·4   5·5

6·2   3·9

CHALLENGE

I am going to reason about different totals. Not all the large numbers can go in a single row or column.

Reflect

Which of these numbers is closest to 0·9? Explain your answer.

1·2   0·87   0·08   0·95   1·01

→ Textbook 6C p88

Problem solving – percentages

1 A shop offers a 15% discount on sale items.

A washing machine is usually £280.

How much is the washing machine in the sale?

2 There are 120 children in Year 6.

30% of the children cycle to school.

25% of the children come to school by car.

The rest of the children walk to school.

How many children walk to school?

3 The table shows information about 240 daily flights from a French airport.

Complete the table.

Destination	Number of flights	Percentage of total flights
Other French cities		30%
European cities	132	
Cities outside Europe		

4 1,800 children visited a museum at the weekend. This number was 40% of the total visitors.

How many visitors were there altogether?

5 Complete the statement.

CHALLENGE

35% of 180 = 30% of ☐

Reflect

Explain how you know that the shaded part of each shape represents 60%.

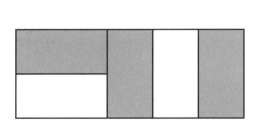

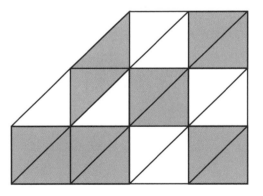

Problem solving – ratio and proportion

1 There are 5 pencils and 3 pens in a box.

a) What fraction of the box is pens?

$$\frac{\boxed{}}{\boxed{}}$$ of the box is pens.

b) Mr Jones buys 9 of these boxes for his class.

How many fewer pens will he have than pencils?

2 A recipe uses 250 g of flour and 75 g of sugar to make 6 cakes.

a) How many cakes can be made using 375 g of sugar?

b) How much flour is needed to make 15 cakes?

3 Here are two rectangles.

Write the ratio of side a to side b.

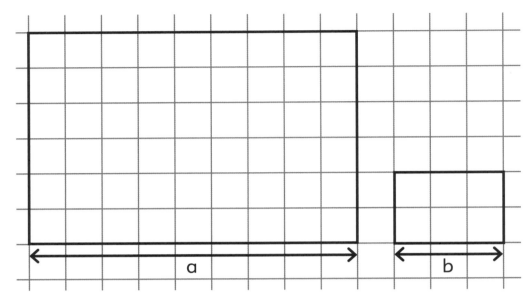

a : b = ☐ : ☐

4 On a map, I cm represents 50 km.

The distance between two cities is 650 km.

0   50   100   150   200

On the map, what is the distance between the two cities?

5 $\frac{3}{8}$ of the children in a tennis club are boys.

What is the ratio of boys to girls?

6   8 small tins have the same mass as 5 large tins.

The mass of a small tin is 350 g.

What is the mass of a large tin?

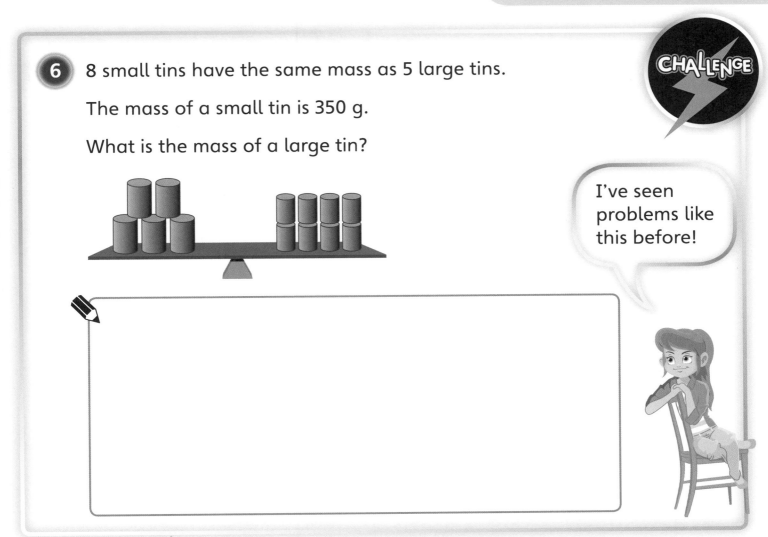

CHALLENGE

I've seen problems like this before!

Reflect

For every 3 strawberry sweets there are 5 lime sweets in a bag.

Explain the steps to work out the number of lime sweets if there are 24 strawberry sweets.

→ Textbook 6C p96

Problem solving – time ❶

1 The time line shows television programmes on 23 June.

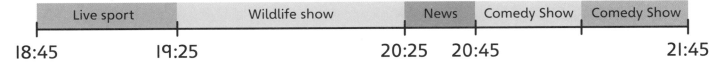

| Live sport | Wildlife show | News | Comedy Show | Comedy Show |

18:45   19:25   20:25   20:45   21:45

a) Max arrives home at 4:20 pm. How long must he wait for the start of the live sport?

b) The two comedy shows are the same length.

Jen watches the news and one comedy show. How long does Jen watch TV for?

c) The next episode of the wildlife show is not until 2 September.

How many **full** weeks must viewers wait?

2 A teacher makes appointments to meet with parents. Each appointment is 20 minutes long. There is a quarter of an hour break each evening.

On Tuesday, appointments start at 15:50 and end at 19:45.

On Wednesday, there are 10 appointments starting at 16:20.

a) How many appointments does the teacher make in total?

b) What time does the last appointment end on Wednesday?

3 Olivia takes part in a fun walk for charity.

She raises £8 for every full hour that she walks. She walks from 10:30 am until 4:15 pm.

How much money does she raise?

4 Which is longer, 12 intervals of 45 minutes or one third of a day?

Explain your answer.

_____

_____

5 **a)** A puppy has lived for 2,904 hours. How many days is this?   **CHALLENGE**

b) Today is 16 October. On what date was the puppy born?

Reflect

The time is twenty-five minutes to 7 in the evening. Explain how to write the time 3 hours 35 minutes later in three different ways.

_____

_____

_____

Problem solving – time ❷

1 Here is part of a bus timetable.

Greytown	14:12	14:42	15:12	15:42	16:12
Oak Street	14:35	↓	15:35	16:05	↓
Ticebridge	14:53	15:20	15:53	16:23	16:50
Bankside	15:20	15:47	16:20	16:50	17:17
Chilhurst	15:45	16:12	16:45	17:15	17:42

a) How many minutes shorter is the journey from Greytown to Chilhurst on the 16:12 bus than on the 15:12 bus?

b) Max arrives at the bus stop in Oak Street at 14:39. He wants to get to Bankside as soon as possible.

Is it quicker for him to walk 38 minutes to Ticebridge or to wait for the next bus at Oak Street?

2 This time line shows a school day.

| Lessons | Break | Lessons | Lunch Break | Lessons |

8:45 am   10:15 am 10:35 pm   12:25 pm   1:20 pm   3:30 pm

How much more time do children spend in lessons than on breaks?

3 The line graph shows a journey Mr Lopez made in his car.

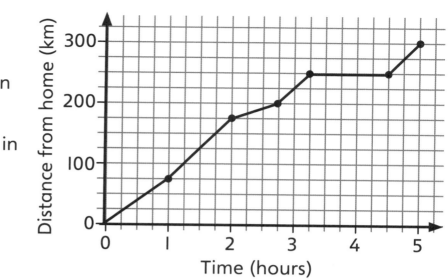

a) How far did he travel in the first 90 minutes?

b) He stopped for a lunch break. How long was this break?

c) Mr Lopez left home at 09:50. What time did he stop for lunch?

4 The table shows the costs of some taxi journeys. The taxi companies charge per minute.

Taxi company	Departure time	Arrival time	Cost
A	10:10 am	10:35 am	£15
B	11:50 am	12:05 pm	£9·75
C	12:10 pm	12:15 pm	£3·20

Max wants to go on a 30 minute journey. Which taxi company will be the cheapest?

Reflect

Lexi says: 'The time is 12:45. In 1 hour 55 minutes it will be 14:00.'

What mistake has she made? What is the correct answer?

77

→ Textbook 6C p104

Problem solving – position and direction

1 The points A, B, C and D are equally spaced along the line AD.

What are the coordinates of B and D?

B(⬚ , ⬚)

D(⬚ , ⬚)

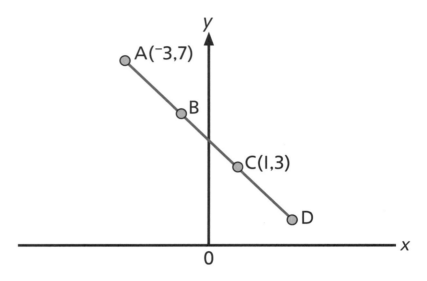

2 **a)** Reflect the rhombus in the y-axis. Use a ruler.

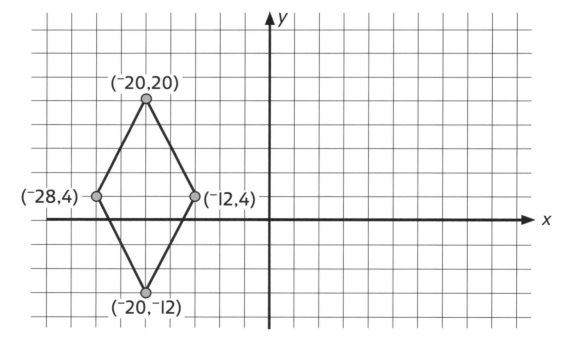

b) Write the coordinates of the vertices in the reflected shape.

(⬚ , ⬚)   (⬚ , ⬚)   (⬚ , ⬚)   (⬚ , ⬚)

78

3 This trapezium is reflected in a mirror line.

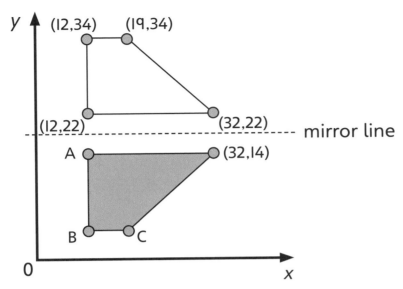

a) What are the coordinates of vertices A, B and C in the reflected shape?

A(⬚ , ⬚)　　B(⬚ , ⬚)　　C(⬚ , ⬚)

b) What are the coordinates of the point half-way between A and B?

(⬚ , ⬚)

c) Circle the coordinates that are inside the reflected shape.

(12,16)　　　(32,12)　　　(22,2)　　　(16,12)　　　(16,15)

4 The points A and B are two vertices of a right-angled triangle.  **CHALLENGE**

One side of the triangle has been drawn on the grid.

Find four possible positions for the third vertex, C.

Write the coordinates.

(☐ , ☐)
(☐ , ☐)
(☐ , ☐)
(☐ , ☐)

I wonder whether AB is the long side or one of the shorter sides of the triangle.

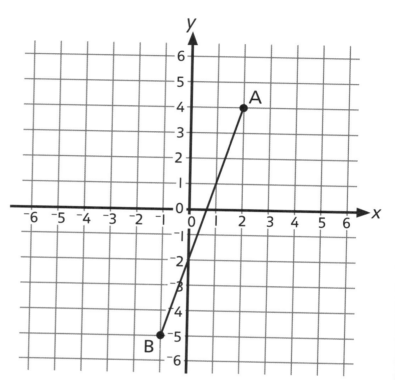

Reflect

Two coordinates (7,2) and (7,10) are plotted on a grid.
Explain how to find the coordinates of the half-way point.

_____

_____

_____

80

Problem solving – properties of shapes ❶

1   Calculate the missing angles in these diagrams.

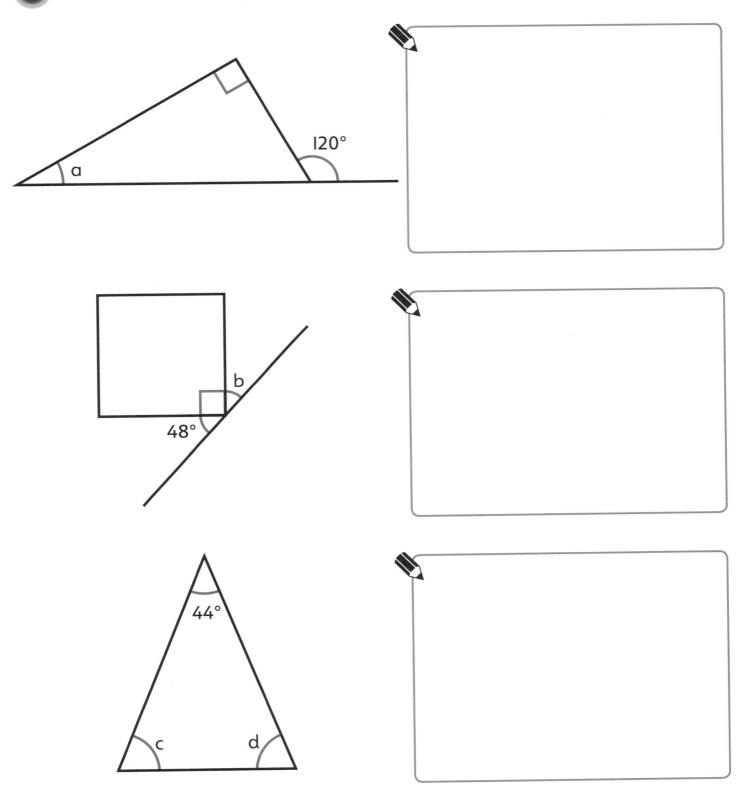

2 **a)** Calculate the sizes of angles a and b.

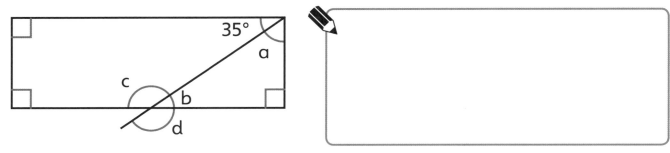

b) Explain how you can now find the sizes of angles c and d.

_____

_____

_____

3 A scalene triangle is drawn inside a square. Calculate the sizes of angles x, y and z.

4 Three angles meet at a point. Angle x is 40° larger than angle y. Angle z is double the size of angle x. What is the size of each angle?

5 Calculate the sizes of angles a, b and c.

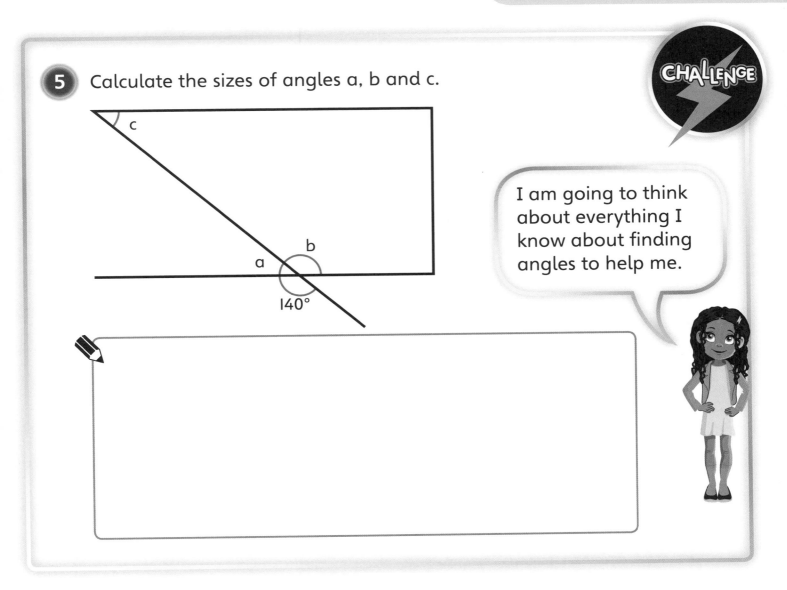

CHALLENGE

I am going to think about everything I know about finding angles to help me.

Reflect

Three angles, a, b and c, are on a straight line. Angle a is **88°**.

What could be the sizes of angles b and c? Find at least two solutions. Explain your answers.

→ Textbook 6C p112

Problem solving – properties of shapes ❷

1 A regular octagon is drawn on a line.

Calculate the size of angle m.

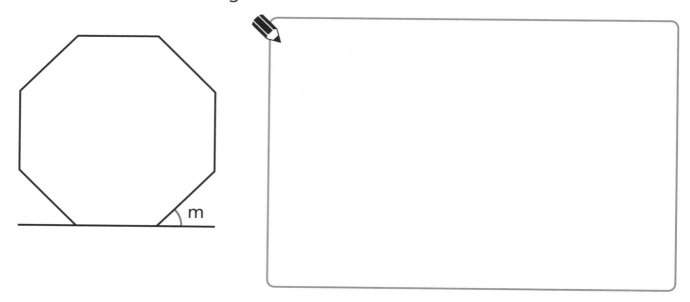

2 Circle all the shapes that are in the wrong section of the table.

Draw an arrow to show which section they should be in.

	Interior angles add up to 360°	Interior angles do not add up to 360°
Have at least one pair of parallel sides	rectangle parallelogram	rhombus regular pentagon
Have no pairs of parallel sides	kite trapezium	triangle regular hexagon

3 Here is a pattern of regular hexagons.

What calculation can you use to prove that the interior angles of three regular hexagons meet around a point?

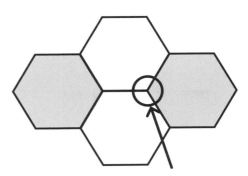

4 Calculate the sizes of angles a and b.

Not drawn to scale

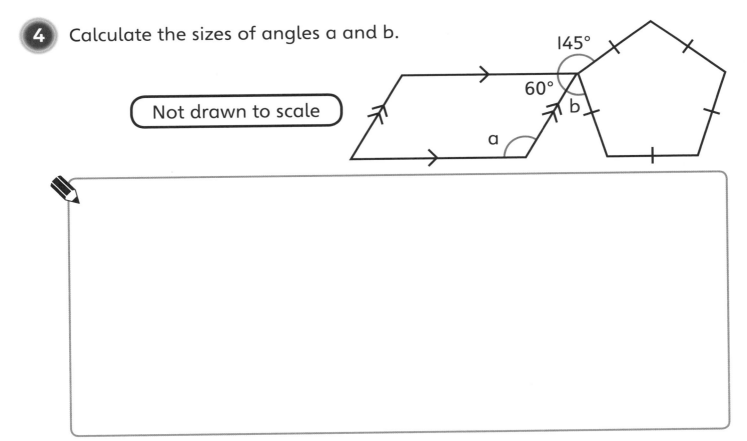

CHALLENGE

5 Max draws an irregular hexagon.

Angles a, b, c and d add up to 600°.

Angle e is double the size of angle f.

Calculate the sizes of angles e and f.

Reflect

Three of the angles in a pentagon add up to to 330°.

Explain how you know that the pentagon is not regular.

End of unit check

My journal

Toshi earns £1,200 a month.

He spends 25% on his rent.

He spends $\frac{3}{10}$ on food and entertainment.

He spends the rest on bills and saves some money too.

For every £3 he spends on bills, he saves £2.

How much will he save in 3 years?

Explain each of your steps. Where did you get stuck?

Power check

How do you feel about your work in this unit?

Power play

I spent three times as much money at the fair as Max but I was there for half the time.

I spent a quarter of the money that Zac spent at the fair. I arrived at 10:30 and left at 13:00.

I spent £10 at the fair. I spent 45 minutes longer at the fair than Jamie.

Jamie

Max

Zac

Complete the table about the children's day at the fair.

	Money spent	Arrival time	Departure time
Jamie			14:15
Max			
Zac		11:15	

Write a similar problem about two or three characters. Give it to a partner to solve. Remember – you need to have worked out the answer!

→ Textbook 6C p122

The mean

1 **a)** Draw three new towers that show the mean height of these three towers.

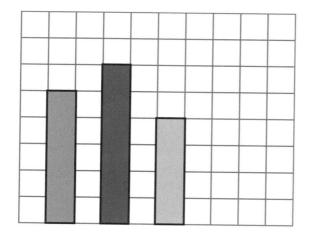 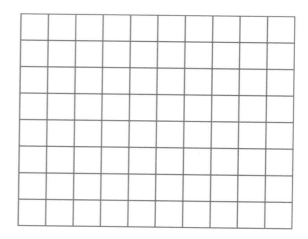

b) Draw four new rows of counters that show the mean length.

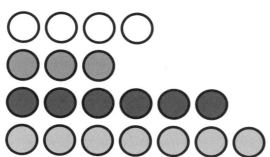 

2 What is the mean number of marbles in the bags?

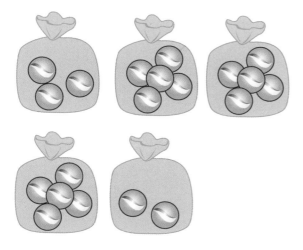 

3 Match groups of dice that have the same mean number of dots.

A

C

B

D

4 Calculate the mean of each set of measurements.

a) 10 cm, 20 cm, 30 cm, 40 cm [   ]

b) 100 ml, 200 ml, 300 ml, 400 ml [   ]

c) 101 kg, 201 kg, 301 kg, 401 kg [   ]

5 Circle the group with the greatest mean.

A [4][1][1][2]

C [2][0][1][0][1][0][0][0]

B [2][0][0][2]

D [1][0][1][0][1][0][1]

6 Find the mean of the two numbers shown on each number line and mark the mean on the number line.

CHALLENGE

a)

100   200

b)

2,000   4,000

c)

198   202

d)

0   7

Explain what you notice.

_____

_____

_____

Reflect

Describe two ways to find the mean of these numbers: 4, 5 and 6.

_____

_____

_____

The mean ❷

1 Complete the bar models to show the mean number of dots on each group of dice.

a)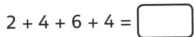

2	4	6	4

$2 + 4 + 6 + 4 = \boxed{}$

$\boxed{} \div 4 = \boxed{}$

b)

I	5	6	2

c)

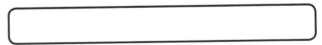

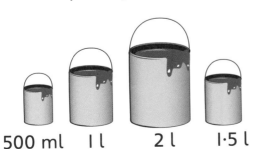

2 Find the mean capacity of these paint pots.

500 ml   I l   2 l   I·5 l

3 These tables show how much money two families spend on food each week.

Which family has the greater mean weekly spend?

Brown Family		
Week 1	Week 2	Week 3
£74	£85	£69

Kapoor Family			
Week 1	Week 2	Week 3	Week 4
£72	£70	£81	£78

4 Find the mean length of all the planks of wood.

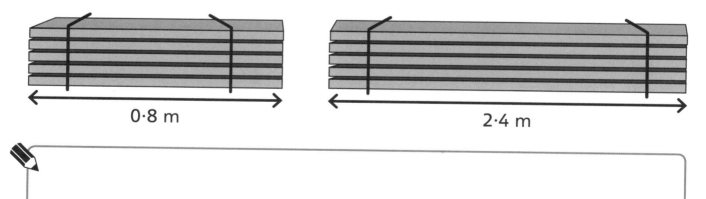

0·8 m   2·4 m

5 Here are the scores from a gymnastics competition.
The winner is the person with the greatest mean score.
Who comes first, second and third?

Kate	5	5·5	5	5·5	–
Amelia	5	5	6	6	5
Lexi	4	8	10	–	–
Bella	0	10	10	10	2

First: _____ Second: _____ Third: _____

Reflect

Complete this sentence.

To find the mean of a set of numbers, you ...

_____

_____

→ Textbook 6C p130

The mean ❸

1 Draw another tower in each group so that the mean height of both groups is 5.

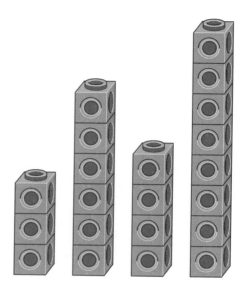

2 The mean number of pets the children have is 4.

How many pets does Emma have?

Bella	2 pets
Andy	12 pets
Danny	1 pet
Emma	

4	4	4	4

3 Four stalls collect money at a cake sale. The mean amount of money collected is £1·50. How much did the fourth group collect?

4 The mean of these sets of number cards is 2·5. What could the missing numbers be?

a)

| 2 | 3 | 3 | |

b)

| 2 | 3 | 3 | | |

5 Draw the water level in Jugs B and E so that the mean volume is $\frac{1}{4}$ litre.

6 Find a solution to each set of clues.

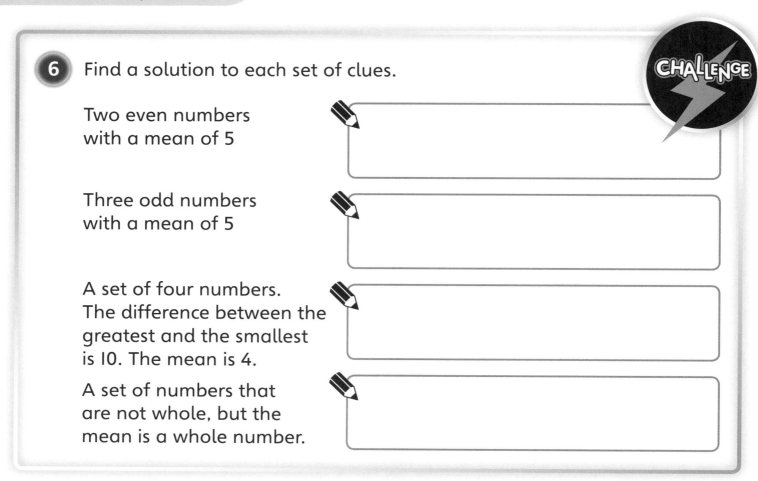

CHALLENGE

Two even numbers
with a mean of 5

Three odd numbers
with a mean of 5

A set of four numbers.
The difference between the
greatest and the smallest
is 10. The mean is 4.

A set of numbers that
are not whole, but the
mean is a whole number.

Reflect

Draw two different sets of number cards which each have a mean of 7·5.
Explain your choice of numbers.

Introducing pie charts

1 These pie charts show three after-school clubs. In which club do more than half the children play football?

Club A   Club B   Club C

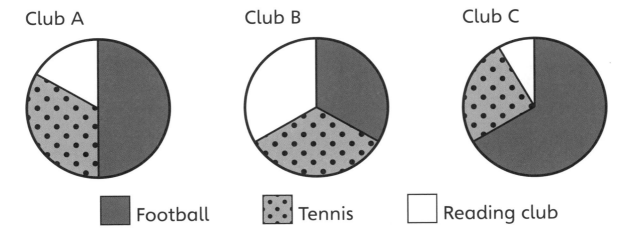

⬛ Football   ⬛ Tennis   ☐ Reading club

More than half the children in Club ____ play football.

2 Children in a class did a survey to find out which jobs they wanted to do when they were older.

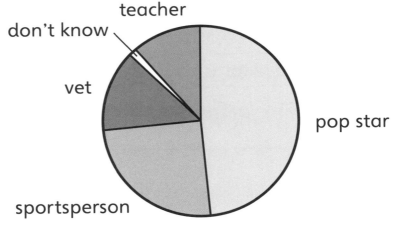

Tick to show whether each statement is true or false.

	True	False
Less than half want to be a pop star.		
The least popular job is vet.		
More children want to be a sportsperson than a teacher.		

3 Match the pie charts to the correct team's set of results.

Team A	
Win	15
Lose	10
Draw	5

Team B	
Win	5
Lose	10
Draw	15

Team C	
Win	10
Lose	10
Draw	10

Team D	
Win	15
Lose	0
Draw	15

4 This tally chart shows the favourite subjects of children in one class. Shade in the sections in the pie chart and complete the key, based on the information in the tally chart.

Subject	Maths	Science	English
Number of students	﹣﹣﹣﹣	﹣﹣	﹣﹣

Number of students — Maths: HH HH IIII — Science: HH II — English: HH HH

Key

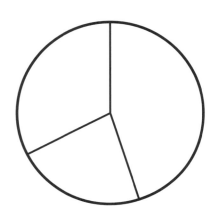

5 The following charts show the different ways people travel to work.

CHALLENGE

cycle

walk

train

car

120
110
100
90
80
70
60
50
40
30
20
10
0

car   walk train cycle

Write questions that can be answered most efficiently using each chart.

Questions to be answered using a pie chart:

_____

_____

Questions to be answered using a bar chart:

_____

_____

Reflect

Describe the differences between a bar chart and a pie chart. When would you use one or the other?

Reading and interpreting pie charts

1 Complete the pie charts to represent the information.

a) Children in a class investigated favourite smoothie flavours.

Flavour	Vote
Banana	卌
Kiwi	l
Strawberry	llll

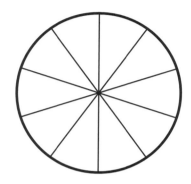

b) This chart shows the children's favourite flavours of ice cream.

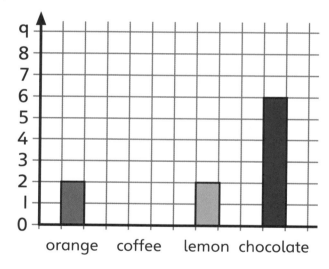

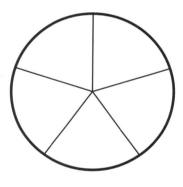

c) 18 people were asked what pets they owned.

Three more people had dogs than rabbits.
The rest had cats.

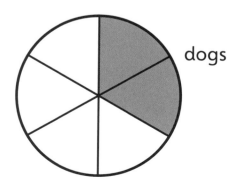

dogs

2 **a)** The pie charts show the games that each team has won, lost and drawn. They receive 3 points for each win, and I point for each draw. How many more points does the best team have than the worst?

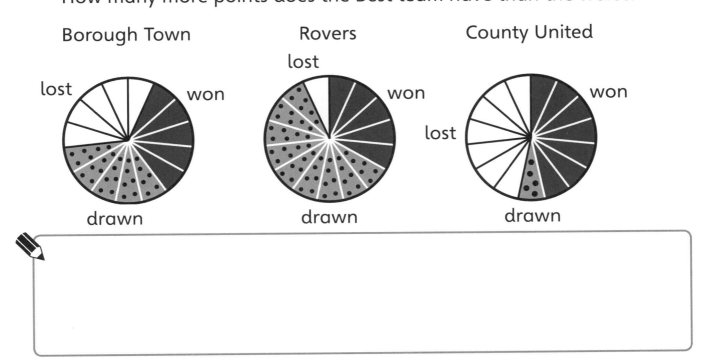

Borough Town   Rovers   County United

b) Eagle United have won 16 points. Complete the pie charts to show three possible sets of results. They received 3 points for a win and I point for a draw.

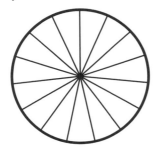 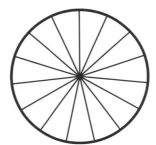 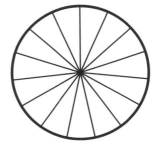

3 800 people were asked if they played video games. Complete and label the pie chart to show what they said.

200 people play once a week.

150 people play every day.

200 people sometimes play.

250 people never play.

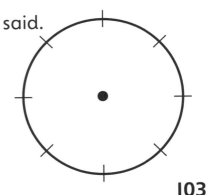

103

4 There are two classes in Year 6. These pie charts show the number of girls and boys in each class.

6a

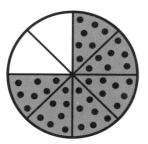

32 children in the class

6b

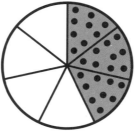

28 children in the class

Key

 Boys

☐ Girls

Complete the pie chart to show the boys and girls in Year 6 altogether.

Children in Year 6

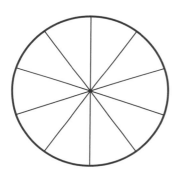

Reflect

Explain how you can work out what each segment of a pie chart represents.

Fractions and pie charts

1. The shaded part of these pie charts show how much time a horse, a cat and a boy spend sleeping in one day. Complete the missing information.

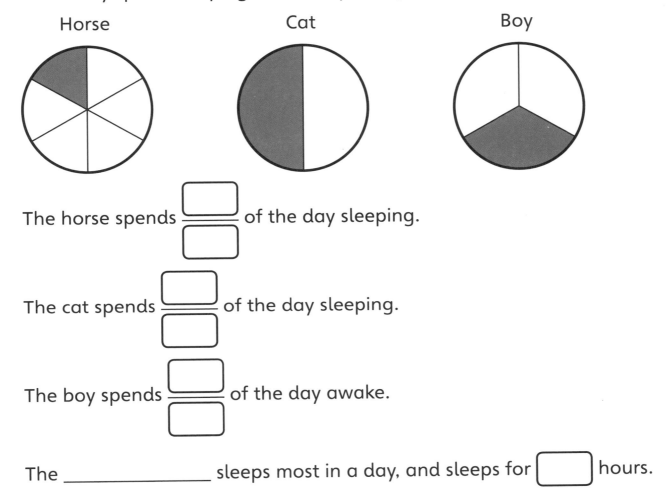

Horse   Cat   Boy

The horse spends ⬜/⬜ of the day sleeping.

The cat spends ⬜/⬜ of the day sleeping.

The boy spends ⬜/⬜ of the day awake.

The _____ sleeps most in a day, and sleeps for ⬜ hours.

2. The pie chart shows the votes for school council representatives. 32 children voted. What fraction of the votes did each child receive?

Jamilla

Isla

Bella

Aki

3 These pie charts represent the number of games two school teams have won, lost and drawn.

Team Tigers
(48 games)

Team Bears
(20 games)

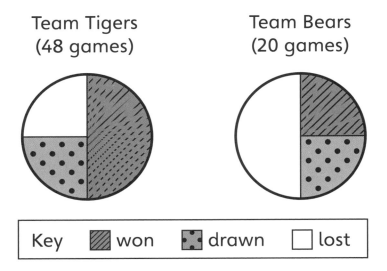

The Tigers have lost more games than the Bears.

Key ▨ won   ⬚ drawn   ☐ lost

Do you agree with Amelia? Explain your answer.

_____

_____

_____

4 Each group voted for their favourite colour. Match each statement to the appropriate pie chart.

21 people chose red

45 people chose black

12 people did not choose yellow

$\frac{1}{3}$ chose red

Group A
(24 people)

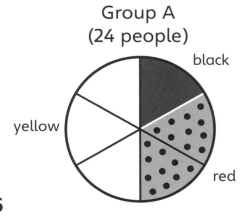

Group B
(30 people)

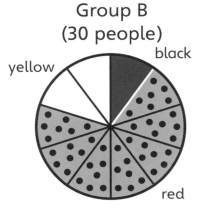

Group C
(180 people)

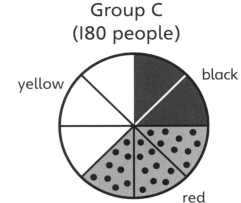

5 A market stall sells dog food, cat food and bird seed. This pie chart shows the sales for one weekend.

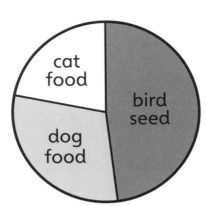

a) Estimate the fraction of the total sales for each type of food.

Show that your fraction estimates add up to I.

b) If the total sales were £300, work out the amount sold for each type of food.

Reflect

What fractions can you see in this pie chart?

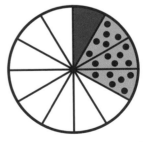

→ Textbook 6C p146

Fractions and pie charts ❷

1 The class looked for different species of tree. Complete the table using the information in the pie chart.

Type of tree	Number seen
birch	
oak	12
pine	
fir	
Total	

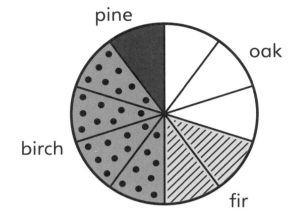

pine

oak

birch

fir

2 There were 24 sightings of sparrows.

a) How many birds were sighted altogether?

b) How many blackbirds were sighted?

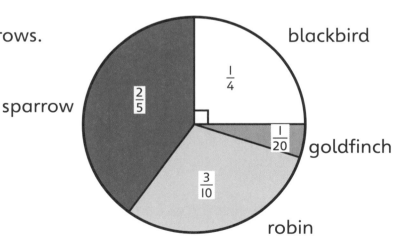

blackbird

sparrow

$\frac{2}{5}$

$\frac{1}{4}$

$\frac{1}{20}$ goldfinch

$\frac{3}{10}$

robin

3 Bella and Max threw beanbags at a target. Bella hit the outer target 28 times. This was two fewer than Max.

Max   Bella

Key

■ missed   ▨ inner target
▨ bullseye □ outer target

Tick the statements that are true. Put a cross against statements that are false.

Bella threw more than 70 times. ☐

Max threw fewer beanbags than Bella. ☐

Bella scored 3 more bullseyes than Max. ☐

4 This pie chart shows which school dinners the children in Class 6 prefer.

What fraction like curry?

96 children like roast dinner. How many children like pizza and curry?

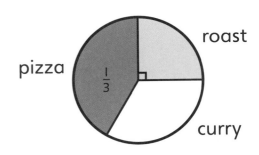

pizza $\frac{1}{3}$ roast

curry

5 This pie chart shows the proportion of ingredients in a tropical fruit drink.

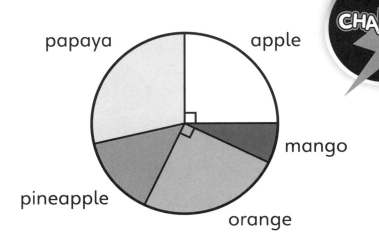

There is twice as much pineapple as mango.

There is twice as much papaya as pineapple.

a) What fraction is mango?

b) In 350 ml of fruit drink, how much more pineapple is needed than papaya?

Reflect

Write a problem for your partner that gives them a fraction of a pie chart, and they have to work out the whole. Sketch a pie chart to go with the problem.

Percentages and pie charts

1 Complete the missing percentages.

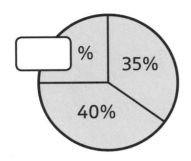 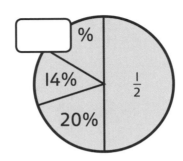 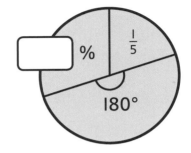

2 60 people voted for a sports captain.

How many votes did each person receive?

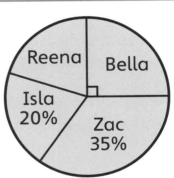

3 This shows the results of a survey about shopping for clothes.

56 people said they go to shopping centres. How many more people shop online than use second-hand shops?

shop online

second-hand shops

25%

35%

shopping centres

4 In one football season, the Rovers scored 48 penalties and missed 32. The pie chart shows what United scored.

Which team was more successful at penalties? Justify your answer.

United penalty kicks

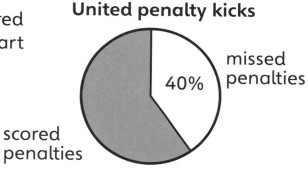

missed penalties

40%

scored penalties

5 These pie charts show the types of tree in Hetiddy Woods and Lanhay Forest.

CHALLENGE

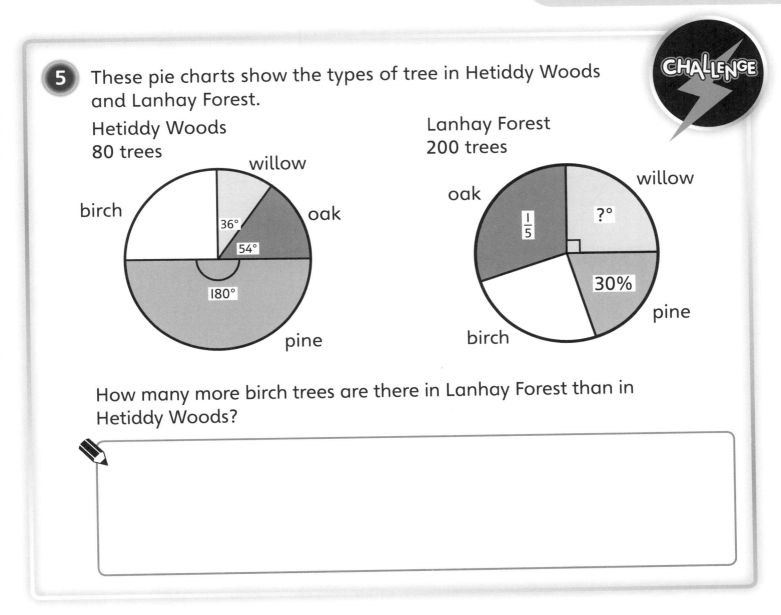

How many more birch trees are there in Lanhay Forest than in Hetiddy Woods?

Reflect

Draw a pie chart that shows $\frac{1}{4}$, 10% and 15%. Show the remaining percentage and explain how you completed this.

Interpreting line graphs

1 The graph shows how the temperature of some tomato sauce cools in the freezer.

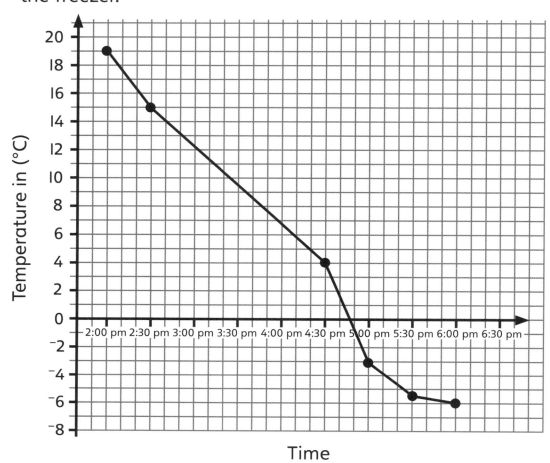

a) What temperature is the tomato sauce at the following times?

2:30 pm ☐ °C

5 pm ☐ °C

b) How much does the temperature decrease between 2 pm and 5:30 pm?

It decreases by ☐ °C.

c) At what time is the temperature of the tomato sauce 0 °C?

☐ : ☐ pm

d) Estimate the temperature of the sauce at 5:45 pm. ☐ °C.

2 Use the graph to estimate the population in each year.

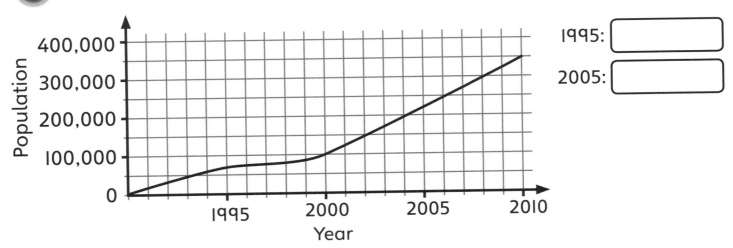

1995: ☐

2005: ☐

3 This graph shows the distance and time for a cyclist travelling in a road race.

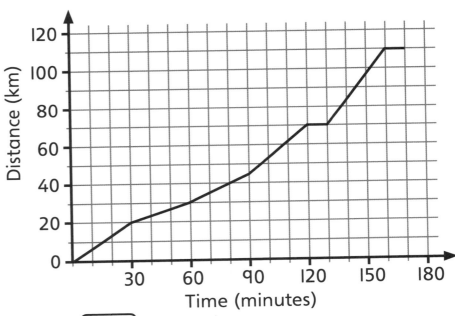

a) How far did the cyclist race? ☐ km

b) Complete the following sentences.

The cyclist slowed to climb a steep hill between ☐ minutes and ☐ minutes.

The cyclist rested for ☐ minutes after ☐ minutes of racing.

After ☐ minutes the cyclist had completed half the distance.

The cyclist raced most quickly between ☐ minutes and ☐ minutes.

115

4 300 runners started a 12 mile race.

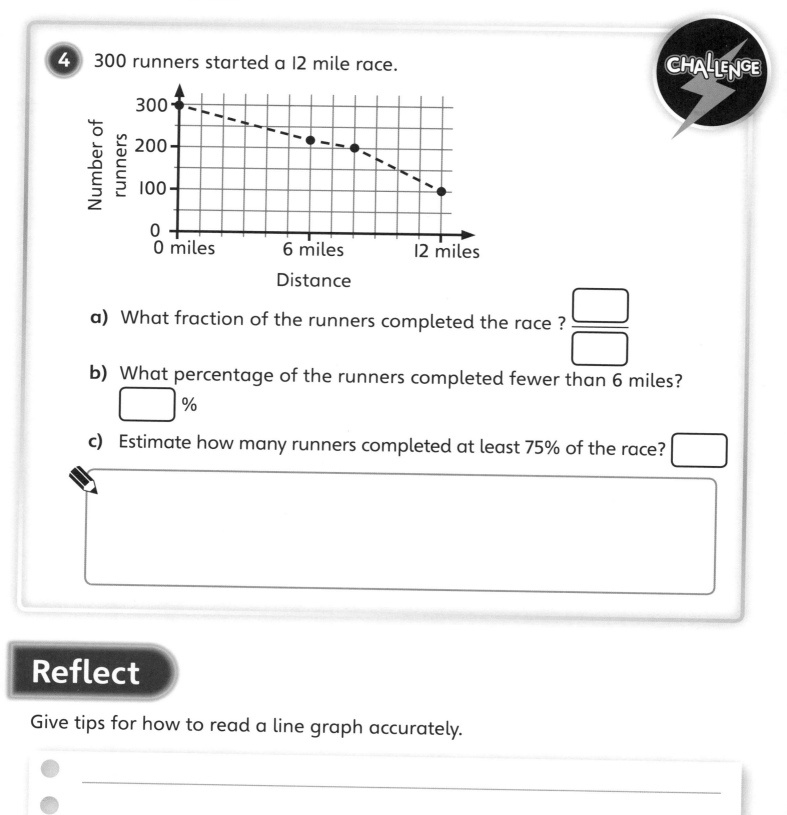

CHALLENGE

a) What fraction of the runners completed the race ?

$\dfrac{\boxed{}}{\boxed{}}$

b) What percentage of the runners completed fewer than 6 miles?

$\boxed{}$ %

c) Estimate how many runners completed at least 75% of the race? $\boxed{}$

Reflect

Give tips for how to read a line graph accurately.

_____

_____

_____

Constructing line graphs

1 Use the information in the table to complete the conversion graph.

Feet	0	2	3	4
Inches	0	24	36	48

Now use the graph to fill in the missing information.

1 foot = ☐ inches

10 feet = ☐ inches

$3\frac{1}{2}$ feet = ☐ inches

$5\frac{1}{4}$ feet = ☐ inches

30 inches = ☐ feet

100 inches = ☐ feet

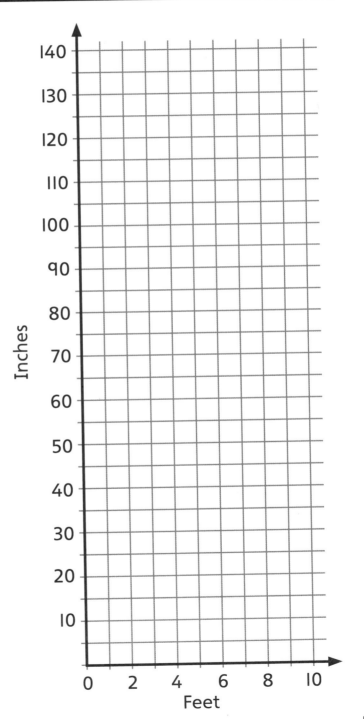

2 These figures show the number of people living in a village over time.

Year	1970	1980	1990	2000	2010	2020
Population	800	1,100	1,500	2,300	3,400	

Use this information to draw a line graph of the population and predict the population in 2020.

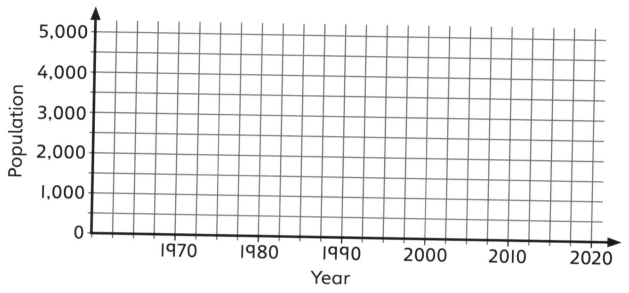

3 These figures show the flight of a firework. Complete the graph from the information, and predict when the firework will land.

Time in seconds	0	2	4	6	8	10	
Height in metres	0	20	30	35	28	15	0

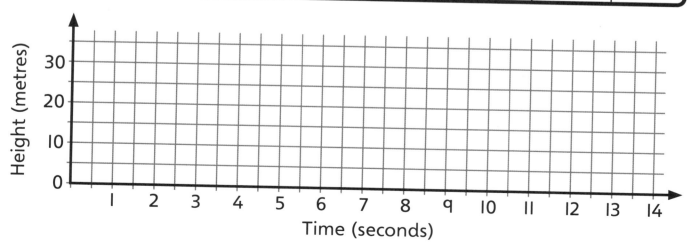

4 Complete the graph to show the conversion between litres and pints.

CHALLENGE

Litres	100	200	300	400	500
Pints	176	354	530		

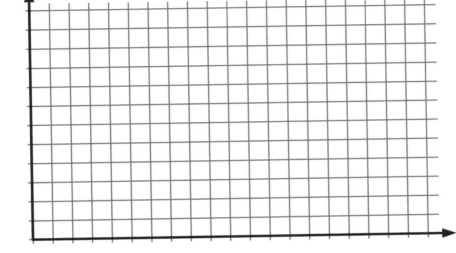

Use the graph to complete the following conversions.

Pints	100		25	
Litres		150		10

Reflect

Explain how you would draw a line graph to convert from metres to kilometres.

→ Textbook 6C p162

End of unit check

My journal

1   Use this information to draw a graph to convert $ (dollars) and £ (pounds). Find the approximate number of £s that equals $19.

Use these numbers: 15 dollars is worth 10 pounds.

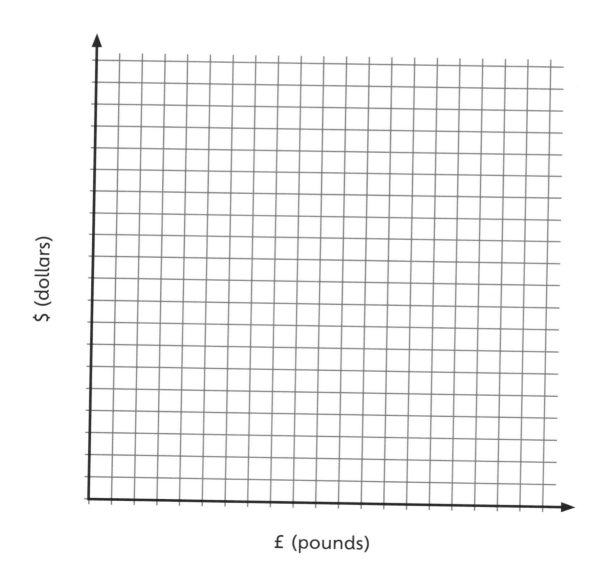

$ (dollars)

£ (pounds)

2 Add notes to this diagram to show when you would use each type of chart, and why its features would be useful.

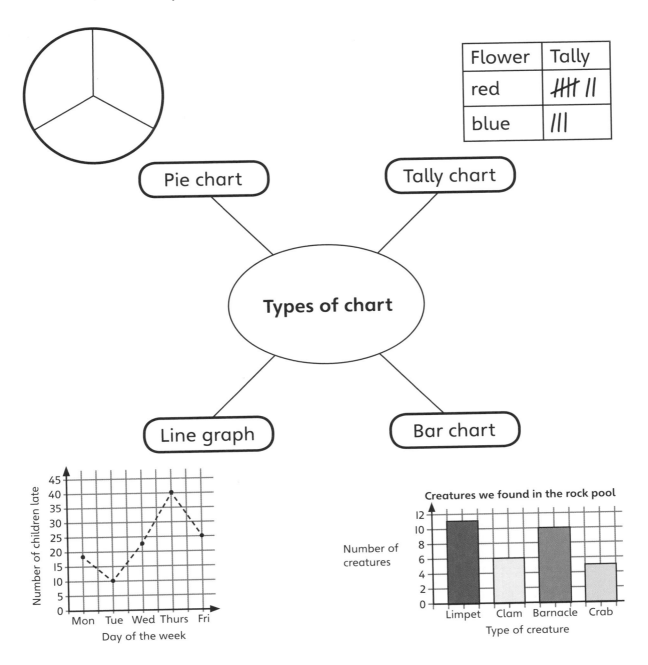

Flower	Tally
red	$\cancel{||||}\ ||$
blue	$|||$

Pie chart

Tally chart

Types of chart

Line graph

Bar chart

Number of children late

45
40
35
30
25
20
15
10
5
0

Mon Tue Wed Thurs Fri
Day of the week

Creatures we found in the rock pool

Number of creatures

12
10
8
6
4
2
0

Limpet Clam Barnacle Crab
Type of creature

Power check

How do you feel about your work in this unit?

Power play

You will need:

- A grid with the *y*-axis going from ⁻50 to 50, and the *x*-axis going from 0 to 20.

How to play:

Play this game with a partner. Choose who is Player 1 and who is Player 2.

Take it in turns to roll two dice. Add the scores on both dice. If the result is an even number, add it to the current score. If the result is an odd number, subtract it from the current score. Each player has 10 turns.

Start at 0. Mark the new score at the turn number on the *x*-axis. Join the points each time you plot a new score to draw a line graph.

Player 1 wins if the line ends as positive. Player 2 wins if the line ends as negative.

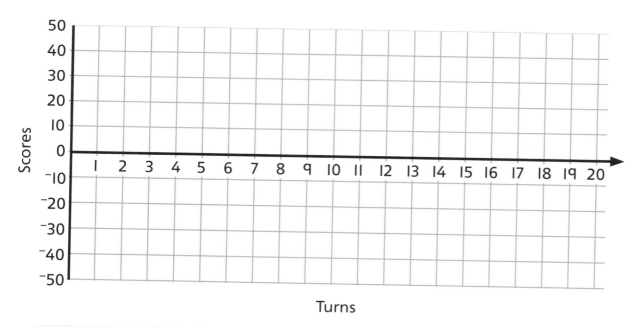

Turns

Draw your own axes and play a few times, but choose different rules. You could multiply the dice or find the difference.

My power points

Put a tick against the topics you have learnt about. Show how confident you are with each one by giving it a number on a scale of 1 to 3.

1 = not at all confident;
2 = getting there;
3 = very confident

Unit 13
I have learnt how to …

☐ Measure angles with a protractor ☐

☐ Draw 2D shapes accurately ☐

☐ Calculate missing angles in triangles and polygons ☐

☐ Calculate missing angles on a straight line ☐

☐ Name parts of a circle, and I know that the diameter is twice the radius ☐

☐ Recognise and draw nets of different 3D shapes ☐

Unit 14
I have learnt how to …

☐ Solve problems about place value ☐

☐ Solve problems involving addition, subtraction, multiplication and division ☐

☐ Solve problems involving fractions and percentages ☐

☐ Solve problems involving lines and angles ☐

☐ Solve problems about time and measurements ☐

☐ Solve multi-step problems ☐

Unit 15

I can ...

☐ Calculate the mean of a group of numbers ☐

☐ Interpret pie charts with fractions, percentages and angles ☐

☐ Interpret line graphs ☐

☐ Create pie charts and line graphs from a set of given facts ☐

Keep up the good work!

Working out

Working out

Squared paper

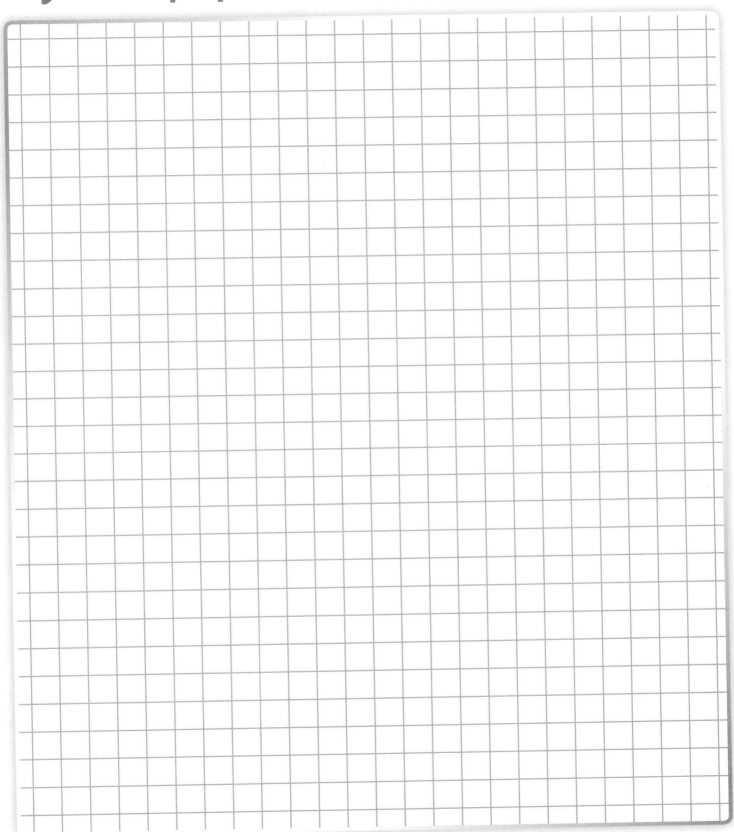

Squared paper